British Military Biplanes
1912–19

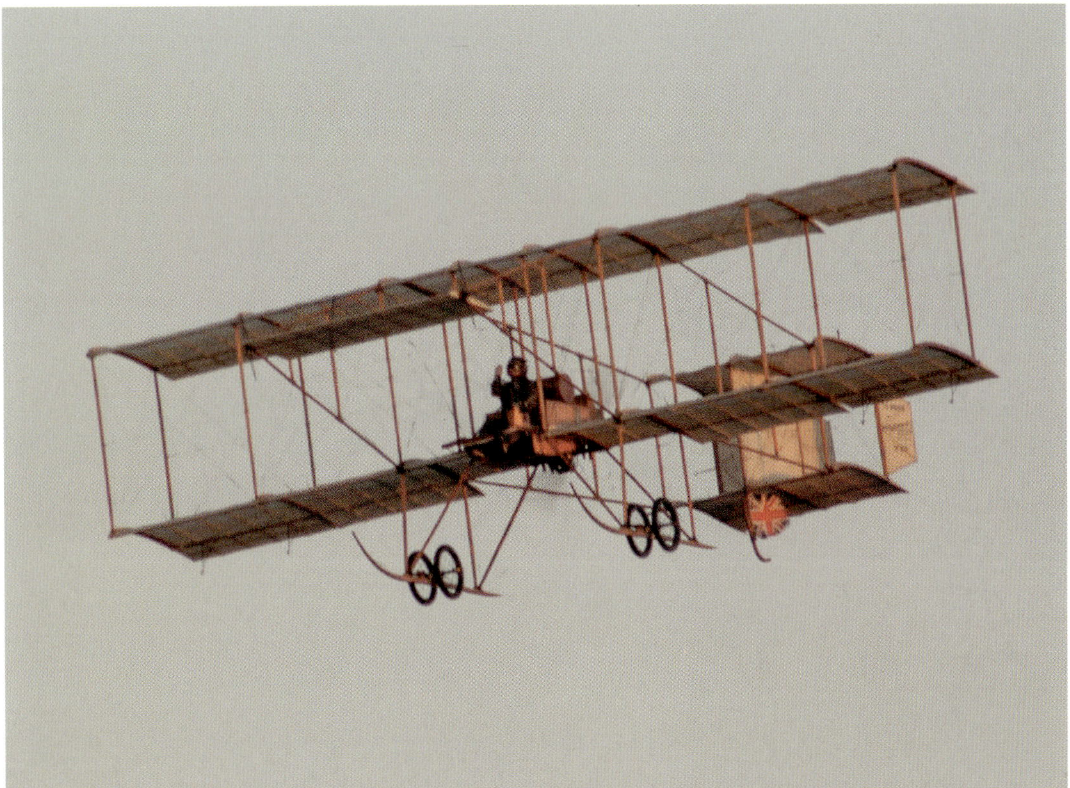

ROGER STAKER

KEY Books

Front cover image: The Sopwith Camel, the Allies' most potent fighter aircraft of the Great War. (Roger Staker)

Title page image: The Bristol Boxkite owed much to early French designs. (Roger Staker)

Contents page image: The Sopwith Pup had 'delightful' flying qualities. (Roger Staker)

Back cover image: Claude Graham-White flies down an avenue in Washington D.C. in his boxkite. (Picryl)

Acknowledgements

The aircraft described in this book are more than 100 years old. Although there are a few original examples in existence and some replicas still flying, most are extinct.

This book would not have been possible without the help and support of a generous community who have provided access to sources of information and research and, most importantly, have kindly allowed the publication of many of the photographs. In addition to the author's own photographs, and those provided by Key Publishing and other sources, special thanks are due to Johan Visschedijk, researcher and co-owner of 1000aircraftphotos.com. His personal collection enabled some potentially large gaps to be filled and he provided access to other collections, enabling the rich variety of photographs contained in this book to be achieved and brought together.

Published by Key Books
An imprint of Key Publishing Ltd
PO Box 100
Stamford
Lincs PE9 1XQ

www.keypublishing.com

The right of Roger Staker to be identified as the author of this book has been asserted in accordance with the Copyright, Designs and Patents Act 1988 Sections 77 and 78.

Copyright © Roger Staker, 2023

ISBN 978 1 80282 599 2

All rights reserved. Reproduction in whole or in part in any form whatsoever or by any means is strictly prohibited without the prior permission of the Publisher.

Typeset by SJmagic DESIGN SERVICES, India.

Contents

Introduction 4

Aircraft in Service 7

Experimental and Prototype Aircraft 122

Alphabetic Index of Aircraft 158

Introduction

On 14 December 1903, Orville Wright made the first ever flight of a 'heavier-than-air' machine, covering a distance of 120ft (36m) in 12 seconds. By the end of the day, both he and his brother Wilbur had managed to extend their flights to 852ft (259m) and maintain a flight time of 59 seconds. Flying had been a human dream for centuries and manned balloon flights took place from the late 1700s. The possibility of heavier-than-air flight had to await the development of internal combustion engines.

If there had been television cameras, the internet and social media in 1903 the whole world would have quickly become aware of the Wright brothers' amazing achievements. But these did not exist and the Wright brothers' claims were widely disbelieved. In October 1906, Alberto Santos-Dumont, a Brazilian living in France, built and flew his Santos-Dumont 14 *bis* aircraft publicly in France. It was Europe's first heavier-than-air flight and many, at that time, thought it was a world first.

In 1908, Wilbur Wright sailed to France with one of his aircraft, giving public performances in that country and in Germany. It is perhaps no surprise that 'copy-cat' designs soon appeared in these countries as well as in the US. The Wright brothers were powerless to stop them. The birth of aviation had taken place.

In Great Britain there had been growing interest in the use of balloons for observation purposes by the army since 1878 and they were used extensively in the Boer War in South Africa between 1899 and 1902. There were obvious limitations due to weather, transportation and the time it took to inflate the balloons. From 1897, what had been known as the School of Ballooning located at Aldershot was renamed the Army Balloon Factory. By 1906, it had moved to Farnborough, a location destined to become a key aeronautical site.

Even in 1907, the army had begun to take note of the advent of powered aircraft. At that time, a Wild West showman, Samuel Franklin Cody (no relation to William 'Buffalo Bill' Cody), was based in England and had helped the army with kites and the development of a dirigible (a steerable airship). For this, he was sent to France where he acquired a 40 horsepower (hp) (30kW) Antoinette engine. He was asked to develop a powered aircraft, which first flew in October 1908, and was recognised as the first flight of such an aircraft in Great Britain.

Louis Bleriot's flight across the English Channel in July 1909 doubtless indicated to many that Great Britain was no longer an island that could be defended solely from the sea.

Interest in this new and exciting sport of flying meant that over the next two years the number of aircraft began to grow, but slowly and in very small numbers. Available machines were primarily of French design, with French engines and there were no established facilities for flying training. It was a risky business and beyond the reach of all but the wealthiest.

Flying machines required engines. The Antoinette engine, designed by French engineer Leon Levasseur and named after his daughter, was the most widely used engine until about 1910. The real breakthrough in engine design was the Gnome rotary engine, designed by the French Seguin brothers in 1908. This engine was the first in a long line of engines of increasing power used in aircraft during the Great War.

Other manufacturers started to build rotary engines, among them the French Le Rhone and Clerget engines were commonly used in Allied fighter aircraft. The Le Rhone engines proved to be reliable

Introduction

and were also built in Great Britain and Italy. British engineering companies also started to develop aero engines. The most famous of these companies was Rolls-Royce. Its in-line Eagle engine was the forerunner of piston aero engines named after birds of prey.

Since 1909, the Army Balloon Factory had been under civilian control and recruited skilled people, including a young Geoffrey de Havilland. He had graduated with an engineering degree and worked in the automotive industry but was fascinated by this new science of flight. The skills required to design and build the early aircraft were largely an understanding of engineering principles and carpentry, given that aircraft structures were made of wood. The Wright brothers were themselves sellers and repairers of bicycles. In 1912, the Army Balloon Factory was renamed the Royal Aircraft Factory.

In a practical sense, the story of British military biplanes began with the creation of the Royal Flying Corps (RFC) on 13 April 1912. As its name implies it was a branch of the British Army. The Navy equivalent, the Royal Naval Air Service (RNAS), was formally announced on 1 July 1914. Until the RFC and RNAS were merged to form the Royal Air Force (RAF) on 1 April 1918, they continued to be military components of the Army and Royal Navy, respectively.

At this time, the Royal Aircraft Factory was renamed the Royal Aircraft Establishment to avoid confusion with the Royal Air Force.

At its launch, the RFC had a complement of fewer than 30 aircraft of varying sorts but mainly of French design. However, among their number were four Boxkites manufactured in Bristol, the first products of a company that would become a household name in aviation circles. Flying was a new technology and aerodynamics an as-yet undiscovered science, so it is little wonder that many senior military officers viewed it with little enthusiasm, despite perhaps realising there was a potential military use for it.

The Great War began in late July 1914, with Great Britain declaring war on Germany on 4 August. At that point, Britain had 113 military aircraft, France 138, Germany 384, Russia 45 and Austria 36. The need for more, and 'better' military aircraft had never been greater, initially for the key purposes of aerial surveillance and reconnaissance.

The S.E.5A was one of the most famous Allied fighters of the Great War. (Roger Staker)

1914 also marked the birth of the British aviation industry as the demand for aircraft mushroomed. Company names associated with aircraft production that would become familiar to generations of enthusiasts and the general public emerged during, and immediately following, the Great War. These included Avro, de Havilland, Handley Page, Vickers, Supermarine, Fairey and Hawker, and they would become recognised throughout the world as representing the very best of British aviation, with overseas sales and sometimes subsidiary companies being established.

In 1909, Louis Bleriot had crossed the English Channel in a monoplane, a simple aircraft with one set of wings and powered by an engine provided by a motorcycle manufacturer, Alessandro Anzani. The engine was a three-cylinder motor producing 25hp (18.6kW). Only the low total weight of the aircraft, engine, pilot and fuel enabled the flight to take place.

The domination of biplanes (aircraft with two sets of wings) as a genre might seem strange. However, a variety of factors converged to make this apparent paradox logical. Powerplants were increasingly heavy and initially low powered. Construction materials were limited to wood and fabric, with metal mountings and bracing wires. To achieve the lift required to enable flight, a large wing area was required. Add a pilot and, later, weapons and the equation became even more finely balanced. Biplanes were the logical solution. There was nevertheless a disadvantage. The additional wing structures of a biplane created extra drag, which inhibited performance. On the other hand, to generate the same lift from a monoplane would demand a much greater wingspan. This would greatly limit manoeuvrability, a key requirement for a fighter aircraft.

There were, of course, successful monoplane aircraft during the Great War – the Fokker Eindekker of 1915 is perhaps the best known, and it was, in its time, greatly feared. Its brilliant Dutch designer Anthony Fokker developed the capability for its machine gun to fire 'through' the swept arc or orbit of the rotating propeller without striking the blades. The Eindekker dominated the skies to such an extent it became known as the 'Fokker Scourge' until Allied aircraft design caught up. There were also multi-winged aircraft, triplanes and even quadruplanes, but the biplane reigned supreme for 20 years.

This book is in two parts. The first describes most of the biplane aircraft that entered service with the RFC and/or the RNAS during the 1912–19 period. The second part of the book describes many aircraft that were experimental in nature or were prototypes not accepted for military service. Although these aircraft were often one-of-a-kind, they nevertheless have an interesting story to tell. In each case, basic technical information is included, the background to its development, as well as the context in which the aircraft was deployed and its service history.

Aircraft in Service

Bristol Boxkite

The Boxkite was the first aircraft manufactured by the British and Colonial Aeroplane Company, which later became the Bristol Aeroplane Company, and was based at Filton, Bristol.

The Bristol Boxkite was designed in 1910 and based on the French Voisin Zodiac aircraft, which had been flown successfully by Henri Farman, who later formed his own manufacturing company. The Boxkite had its first flight on 30 July 1910. It was designed as a two-seat trainer aircraft with the second seat set higher than the front one. Many early military pilots learned basic flying skills on this type of aircraft.

The aircraft was constructed of ash and spruce and covered with linen, a construction method that evolved for many years until new materials and techniques emerged. The elevator was carried ahead of the aircraft on twin booms. The length of the Boxkite was 38ft 6in (11.73m), and it stood more than 11ft (3.35m) high. The military version had the wingspan extended by 12ft (3.7m) to 46ft 6in (14.17m).

The Le Rhone-manufactured rotary engine of 70hp (52kW) was situated behind the cockpit area and operated in pusher mode. It was mounted on two substantial wooden beams, which continued forward

The Bristol Boxkite. This is a replica built for the 1965 film *Those Magnificent Men In their Flying Machines*. (Roger Staker)

to hold the seats for the pilot and trainee or passenger. The top speed was 40mph (64km/h). Inevitably it would now be considered a slow and clumsy aircraft to fly, but it was of its time and served its purpose as a trainer until more sophisticated machines became available.

In March 1911, the War Office placed an initial order for four Boxkites, two to be powered by 50hp (37kW) Gnome engines and two with 60hp (44.7kW) Renault engines. They equipped the No.2 (Aeroplane) Company of the British Army Air Battalion, which was established at the beginning of April 1911. This was the first contract ever placed for production of an aircraft to serve in Britain's military services. The Boxkite continued in British military service into 1915.

The first overseas government order for the embryo British aviation industry came from Russia. Eight Boxkites were ordered and delivered to St Petersburg in April 1911. These aircraft had the extended 'military' wings and enlarged fuel tanks. They were fitted with Le Rhone rotary engines.

Following the outbreak of the Great War, the RFC ordered four more Boxkites. The last survivor of which was written off in February 1915. Two Boxkites were used by the RNAS, and the Admiralty ordered six for training duties. These remained operational at least until 1915. On 1 March 1914, the first Australian military flight took place when a Boxkite was flown by Lieutenant Harrison. It continued to serve until it was written off in 1917. Two aircraft were exported to India and they flew in several military manoeuvres, but not in any combat situation.

A total of 78 Bristol Boxkite aircraft were constructed, with the extended wing military version accounting for 60 of these. Given the early stage of aviation, and that of the industry, this was a large number of aircraft. Production of the Bristol Boxkite continued until 1914. The final six Boxkites were constructed by Bristol Tramways in Brislington, Bristol

Four Boxkites were deployed by the Central Flying School, a training unit of the Australian Air Force. One of these was built in Australia, making the Boxkite the first military aircraft to be manufactured there.

The Bristol Boxkite landing after an evening flight. (Roger Staker)

Royal Aircraft Factory B.E.2

The B.E.2 family of aircraft first flew on 1 February 1912. Built by the Royal Aircraft Factory at Farnborough, Surrey, it was designed by Geoffrey de Havilland who would be the founder of one of Britain's most successful aircraft manufacturing companies. It was the first conventional aircraft design. The B.E.2 was powered by a 70hp (52kW) Renault air-cooled in-line engine. Many variants of this aircraft were developed over its life cycle.

In August 1912, a B.E.2 obtained the British Altitude Record of 10,560ft (3,219m), flown by Geoffrey de Havilland. In November 1913, a B.E.2 flew non-stop for 650 miles (1,040km), establishing a British record.

During the life of the B.E.2 family, a number of sub-contractors were deployed in its construction, including Vickers Ltd, Handley Page Ltd, British & Colonial Company (later Bristol Aeroplane Company), Messrs Hewlett and Blondeau, G & J Weir of Glasgow, The Coventry Ordnance Works, Blackburn Aircraft Company, and motor manufacturers Austin, Daimler, Armstrong-Whitworth, Napier and Siddeley-Deasy.

The B.E.2, 2a and 2b were two-seat reconnaissance aircraft of unusual design in that there was no wing stagger between the upper and lower wings as there was in later models. These versions were also powered by an air-cooled 70hp (52kW) Renault motor giving the aircraft a maximum speed of 70mph (112km/h). The service ceiling was 10,000ft (3,048m).

These aircraft were constructed of wood, with spruce for the wings, and all surfaces were fabric covered. The wingspan was 38ft 7in (11.77m), and the length 29ft 6in (8.99m).

The B.E.2a was the first production version built from early 1912 and was still in service in late 1914. Control of the wings was through wing-warping as there were no ailerons fitted. The B.E.2b had deeper sides to the cockpit area and the later aircraft had ailerons in place of wing-warping controls.

War in the air was an unknown and unwelcome experience. As reconnaissance aircraft, there seemed to be no need to think about defensive, and even less, offensive armament. Consequently, in the early stages of the war, these aircraft were unarmed and therefore extremely vulnerable to enemy action, but nevertheless the B.E.2 became the first British aircraft to land on the continent of Europe at the outbreak of the Great War in 1914. More than 130 B.E.2, B.E.2a and B.E.2b aircraft were built. They were used primarily for reconnaissance purposes until 1915.

The Royal Aircraft Factory B.E.2b. (Alamy)

Grahame-White Type XV

The Bristol aircraft was not the only Boxkite and similar designs were produced by other manufacturers, often based on French designs such as the Maurice Farman Longhorn and Shorthorn. The Grahame-White Type XV was also often called the Boxkite, although this referred more accurately to an earlier aircraft.

The first flight took place in 1913 and one RFC aircraft was used for the test firing of a Lewis machine gun, the first time a machine gun had been used for firing at a ground target from the air.

The aircraft was manufactured with a pod and boom construction with two seats initially situated side by side on the leading edge of the lower wing, but in later versions these were mounted in tandem with the engine in pusher configuration behind the nacelle. It was used extensively by the RFC and RNAS for training, with 135 aircraft being constructed. The Australian Flying Corps also used the Grahame-White aircraft for training.

Claude Grahame White flying his aircraft in Washington D.C. (Picryl)

Avro 504

One of the most famous British aircraft of all time, the 504 series was designed and built by A. V. Roe in Manchester. The first Avro 504, powered by an 80hp (60kW) Gnome rotary engine, took its maiden flight in 1913. A later variant of the Avro 504, the 504N, remarkably was still in service with the RAF in 1944 and is described in the book *British Military Biplanes: 1920–40*.

In the summer of 1913, the War Office issued an order for 12 Avro 504s for the newly formed RFC. The 504 entered service in 1913.

The name 'Avro' became synonymous with fine British aircraft for more than 70 years. Development of the 504 models from the 504A to the 504K took place from 1914–17, each having basically the same fuselage but with a variety of powerplants and other enhancements. The powerplants included Gnome, Le Rhone, Clerget and Rolls-Royce rotary engines. Depending on the type of powerplant, top speeds varied from 62 to 82mph (99 to 131km/h).

Although intended originally for reconnaissance and light bombing missions, the 504 became the standard trainer. However, it was also deployed as a home defence fighter and was equipped with a single Lewis machine gun mounted above the upper wing. The RFC and the RNAS purchased Avro 504s, and a small number were taken to France at the beginning of the Great War. An Avro 504 was the first British aircraft to be shot down by a German fighter, on 22 August 1914.

The Avro 504A was designed for the RFC with modified wing struts and a reduced wingspan. A total of 1,485 of this version were built. The 504B was a modification, this time for the RNAS. The wing spars

Avro 504B. (Picryl)

were larger and there was a large dorsal fin in front of the 504's classic teardrop- or 'comma'-shaped rudder. In total, 200 of this variation were built. Both models were fitted with 80hp (60kW) Gnome, Le Rhone or Clerget engines.

In an attempt to counter the Zeppelin bombing raids over England, 80 single-seat versions, designated 504C, were built for the RNAS. In place of the observer's space in the aircraft, an additional fuel tank was installed. The 504C had the Gnome engine and the aircraft's endurance was a remarkable eight hours. It had an upward-firing machine gun loaded with incendiary ammunition with the intention of attacking Zeppelins from below.

Another Zeppelin interceptor, this time for the RFC, was the 504D, of which just six were built. This model retained the original rudder profile.

The Avro 504E and the 504F were experimental in that they were fitted with different engines and in the case of the 504E a reduction in the wing stagger. The ten 504Es for the RNAS had 100hp (75kW) Gnome Monosoupape engines, while the single 504F had a 75hp (56kW) Rolls-Royce Hawk in-line engine.

The RNAS received 30 Avro 504Gs, a two-seat weapons-training variant of the 504B. This had twin synchronised forward-firing Vickers machine guns and a Lewis machine gun on a Scarff ring in the rear cockpit. The RNAS also wanted to undertake catapult trials with the 504, and 12 504Cs were converted for this purpose. Both these versions used the 80hp (60kW) Gnome engine.

The first mass-produced version was the Avro 504J, of which 2,070 were constructed. It was a two-seat training aircraft fitted with either a 100hp (75kW) Gnome or an 80hp (60kW) Le Rhone engine.

The most successful and numerous version was the Avro 504K, with nearly 5,000 built. It was designed in recognition of the problems being experienced in 1917 with the supply of rotary engines for the 504s already in service or required for service. Avro 504 aircraft had been built to accommodate a number of specific makes of rotary engines, which entailed unique mountings for each engine type. Replacement for a damaged or unserviceable engine therefore had to be of the same make and model as that originally installed. Intermittent supply problems, inevitable given the heavy demands placed on manufacturers, were preventing aircraft returning to service quickly. The solution was to permit a variety of different interface plates to be fitted, allowing a wide range of rotary engines to be installed but all within a smooth cowling. This widened available engine choices to include Gnome Monosoupape, Le Rhone, Clerget and others.

During the Great War, more than 7,000 trainer versions of the 504 were issued to British training squadrons, but perhaps the most famous operation by Avro 504s came in November 1914, three months after the outbreak of war. Three 504s of the RNAS, equipped with additional fuel capacity and with bomb racks, undertook the world's first strategic bombing raid on the Zeppelin sheds at Friedrichshafen on Lake Constance, Germany. The aircraft took off from Belfort in France, for a 250-mile (400km) flight taking four hours. Two aircraft returned safely, but one was shot down and the pilot became a prisoner of war.

By mid-1915, the Avro 504 was no longer suitable for frontline operations in France and the aircraft was withdrawn. It became the standard training aircraft for both the RFC and the RNAS.

The Avro 504's wings were made of spruce with fabric covering. The fuselage framework was made of ash and was fabric-covered except for the decking near the cockpits, which was covered in three-ply wood. The wingspan was 37ft 6in (11.43m), and the length 29ft 6in (8.99m). The fuel tank could hold 30 imperial gallons (135 litres/36 US gallons) of petrol.

As the Great War ended, there were still 5,446 Avro 504s 'on charge' to British military forces. His Majesty King George VI learned to fly in an Avro 504K. With so many aircraft available for disposal following the cessation of hostilities it is little wonder that the 504 became popular as a civilian aircraft, including the provision of 'joy rides', or 'barnstorming' at local fetes and similar events.

Aircraft in Service

The Avro 504K gave so many their first flight. (Roger Staker)

The Avro 504 was attractive to foreign governments, and after the Great War, military users included Argentina, Australia, Belgium, Brazil, Canada, Chile, China, Denmark, Finland, Guatemala, Ireland, Japan, Mexico, the Netherlands East Indies, New Zealand, Norway, Portugal, South Africa, Spain, Sweden and the US.

The total number of Avro 504s manufactured, of all models, was in excess of 10,000 including those built overseas. Of these, about 8,970 were constructed during the Great War, making the Avro 504 the most produced military aircraft of the Great War. Manufacturing of 504s took place in Australia, Canada, Argentina, Japan, Belgium and Mexico.

An Avro 504K showing its anti-nose-over ski. (Roger Staker)

Bristol T.B.8

The Bristol Aeroplane Company's Chief Designer, Henri Coanda, modified the design of his earlier monoplane aircraft to produce a two-seat biplane called the Bristol T.B.8. It was designed in response to an order from the Admiralty. The first aircraft flew in August 1913 and the T.B.8 was tested with both a wheeled undercarriage and with floats. The T.B.8 was purchased by the RNAS and RFC.

Its powerplant was typically an 80hp (60kW) seven-cylinder Gnome Lambda or 80hp (60kW) Le Rhone rotary engine giving a maximum speed of 65mph (104km/h), although a variety of rotary engines were installed in T.B.8s ranging from 50hp (37kW) Gnome to 100hp (75kW) Gnome Monosoupape engines.

Although the endurance was five hours, the rate of climb was slow, taking 11 minutes to reach 3,000ft (914m). Its wingspan was 37ft 8in (11.48m), and its length 29ft 3in (8.92m).

T.B.8s entered service in late 1913 and were primarily used in a training role, although a few could carry light bombs. At the outbreak of the Great War, the RFC transferred its complement of T.B.8s to the RNAS. On 25 November 1914, a Bristol T.B.8 undertook a bombing mission against a German artillery battery at Middelkerke, West Flanders. There is no indication that other bombing raids by T.B.8s were carried out.

The early aircraft used wing warping for lateral control, but later models were equipped with ailerons.

The aircraft was soon relegated to training roles because its performance was inadequate for frontline operations. It continued as a trainer until 1916.

Henri Coanda was Romanian, so it is perhaps no surprise that the Romanian government should express an interest in the Bristol T.B.8. It placed an order for an enhanced version, with a more powerful engine and other aerodynamic changes. Although the aircraft was ready in mid-1914, it was never delivered to Romania and was requisitioned by the RFC.

A total of 54 Bristol TB.8 aircraft were built.

The Bristol T.B.8 was not suitable for operational purposes. (Picryl)

Sopwith Three-Seater

Thomas Sopwith learned to fly in 1910. His interest in aviation having been stimulated, he established a flying school at Brooklands, Surrey. Here he built a biplane using the wings from a Wright biplane and a fuselage and tail from an early Coventry Ordnance Works aircraft. He called it the Hybrid and it first flew on 4 July 1912. It was rebuilt in October, sold to the Admiralty and delivered in November 1912.

The Admiralty was clearly impressed as it issued a tender for an improved aircraft based on Sopwith's design. In response, Thomas Sopwith established the Sopwith Aviation Company with a factory in Kingston-upon-Thames.

The aircraft that emerged was the Sopwith Three-Seater, also known as the Sopwith D.1. Lateral control was by wing warping and it was powered by an 80hp (60kW) Gnome Lambda rotary engine. There were two open cockpits. The passengers sat side-by-side in the front cockpit while the pilot occupied the rear cockpit. Three transparent windows made of celluloid were fitted to each side of the fuselage to provide a downwards view.

Sopwith retained the second aircraft as a demonstrator. The aircraft established new altitude records in June and July 1913.

The RNAS ordered another two aircraft, which were delivered by September 1913. The RNAS took three to France at the outbreak of war. Although the aircraft were mainly used for reconnaissance missions, attempts were made to conduct bombing raids on Zeppelin sheds and railways. They were withdrawn in October 1914. One was used for patrol duties on the east coast of Britain until November 1915.

Once ailerons were fitted in place of wing warping, the RFC ordered nine aircraft in September 1913. They were received by March 1914, but due to accidents only a few were still airworthy by August, and these were used for training in Britain.

The Three-Seater had a maximum speed of 74mph (119km/h) and a service ceiling of 12,900ft (3,900m), but this was achievable with only one passenger on board. The wingspan was 40ft (12.19m) and the length was 29ft 6in (8.99m).

The Sopwith Three-Seater. (Picryl)

Short S.38

In early 1910, the Short Brothers embarked on the construction of an aircraft designed by Horace Short and based on the French Farman III pusher. It was almost identical to the Bristol Boxkite of the same era, and was called the Short S.27.

This aircraft suffered a serious accident when being hoisted onto a ship. It was returned to Short Brothers, which rebuilt it with a similar layout, but with a nacelle for the two crew members and with improvements to the tailplane and rudders. It was first flown on 30 August 1912.

Nine production aircraft were built by Short and delivered to the RNAS; some remained in service after the outbreak of the Great War for coastal patrol and training purposes. In 1915, the RNAS wanted more S.38 aircraft, but Short was busy with other aircraft so the construction was sub-contracted to Pemberton-Billing Ltd, and White and Thompson. Deliveries of the S.38 continued into 1916 and the type remained in service until 1917.

Powered by a Gnome Lambda air-cooled radial engine, the S.38 had a top speed of 58mph (93km/h) and a range of 290 miles (464km). Its wingspan was 52ft (16m) and its length was 35ft 6in (10.82m).

Short S.38. (Picryl)

Royal Aircraft Factory B.E.8

The B.E.8 was a product of the Royal Aircraft Factory and was the last of the B.E. series of aircraft fitted with a rotary engine, later aircraft having in-line motors. Its design dates from 1912. Three prototypes were built at the Royal Aircraft Factory in Farnborough in 1912 and 1913, but all eventual production machines were constructed by sub-contractors.

The B.E.8 was a two-seat general purpose and reconnaissance machine, with many of its airframe components 'borrowed' from the B.E.2. A total of 70 aircraft were constructed, but only small numbers were used over the Western Front from 1914, the remainder being largely relegated to training roles through to 1916. As might be expected, its construction was wood with fabric covering. The wingspan was 37ft 8in (11.48m) and its length was just over 27ft 4in (8.33m).

The B.E.8 was powered by a seven-cylinder Gnome Lambda rotary engine generating 80hp (60kW). This gave the aircraft a maximum speed of 70mph (112km/h), and it had an endurance of only 90 minutes. It took more than ten minutes to climb to 3,000ft (914m). In common with other British military aircraft at the beginning of the Great War, there was no fixed armament although some crew members carried small arms. Small bombs to a total weight of 100lb (45kg) could be accommodated.

The design was unusual in that it had a large double cockpit rather than two separate cockpits. This did not find favour with the RFC and production models were built with two cockpits.

The B.E.8 reconnaissance aircraft. (Picryl)

Sopwith Tabloid Scout

The Sopwith Tabloid Scout (the title normally given to fighter aircraft during the Great War) took its first flight on 27 November 1913. When it was demonstrated it caused a sensation. Its performance outclassed any biplane of the time irrespective of country of origin. With a Gnome Lambda rotary engine producing 80hp (60kW), it had a top speed of 92mph (147km/h). Although constructed conventionally of wood with fabric covering, the engine was almost completely enclosed in an aluminium cowling, giving the aircraft a surprisingly streamlined appearance. There were just two small air intake holes and an exhaust outlet at the base of the cowling. The Tabloid used wing-warping for lateral control.

It was designed by Thomas Sopwith and Fred Sigrist and was demonstrated by Harry Hawker, who would eventually establish the famous aircraft manufacturing company in his name. The name Tabloid is alleged to have arisen because of the aircraft's small dimensions – like a tabloid newspaper. Alternatively, it may have been named after a square-shaped compact medical kit, popular at the time. The Tabloid's wingspan was 25ft 6in (7.77m), and it was just 20ft (6.1m) long.

The high performance of the Tabloid encouraged Sopwith to enter the annual Schneider Trophy Air Race. A specially converted seaplane version was built, powered by an 100hp (75kW) Gnome Monosoupape engine, which Thomas Sopwith personally collected from Paris. The aircraft was flown at Monaco where it succeeded in winning the 1914 Schneider Trophy race for Britain. It was the first British-designed-and-built aircraft to win a major international trophy.

Some historians contend that the supremacy of the Tabloid over what were then emerging as 'rival' monoplanes ensured the supremacy of biplanes for the next 20 years.

The surprisingly streamlined Sopwith Tabloid. (Picryl)

The first Tabloid for the RAF was delivered in 1914 and has the distinction of being the first single-seat scout/fighter to enter service. As was common to other single-seat British aircraft of the time, there were no fitted armaments. However, during the early part of 1915, some pilots carried rifles, pistols and other weapons. Eventually some machines were fitted with a machine gun, but in the absence of propeller interrupter systems, the aircraft had to be flown in a crab-like manner in order for it to be used.

Tabloids were issued to two squadrons on the Western Front and a small number were deployed to the RNAS. Three of these were used for attacks on German targets. On 8 October 1914, two Tabloids flying from Antwerp destroyed Zeppelin Z.IX in its hangar at Dusseldorf and bombed Cologne railway station. Four Tabloids embarked on HMS *Ark Royal* in 1915 for the Dardanelles.

A total of 35 Sopwith Tabloids were produced.

The streamlined nose of the Sopwith Tabloid is very clear here. (Picryl)

Vickers F.B.5 Gunbus

The Vickers F.B.5 Gunbus was developed as a way of providing a means of delivering straight-line fire power without the need for interrupter gear. It was a simple solution: mount the powerplant at the rear of the fuselage using a pusher layout. Vickers was not alone in applying this simple solution.

By early 1915, what had been a mobile war had ground to a halt across parts of Belgium and Eastern France. All the warring armies dug in, literally, creating an unbroken line of trenches that ran from the Belgian coast to the border with Switzerland. The Western Front had been created. For the British Army, the hope of a war in which the cavalry would play a dominant role had been dashed. The war would, for the foreseeable future, be dominated by artillery, underground mines and foot soldiers. The only mobility available was in the air. Reconnaissance, observation of the opposition's activities and support for artillery targeting were now key functions that could only be undertaken from the air.

Obstruction of the enemy's ability to undertake these activities also became a major focus of military intention. The relatively new role of the fighter aircraft became ever more important. The F.B.5 Gunbus was arguably the first purpose-built fighter aircraft to see service.

It was recognised that the pusher layout was not the most efficient from a performance point of view but the absence of a synchronised interrupter gear (to allow firing through the rotating propeller for the machine gun) made this the only practical solution to the German challenge in the air.

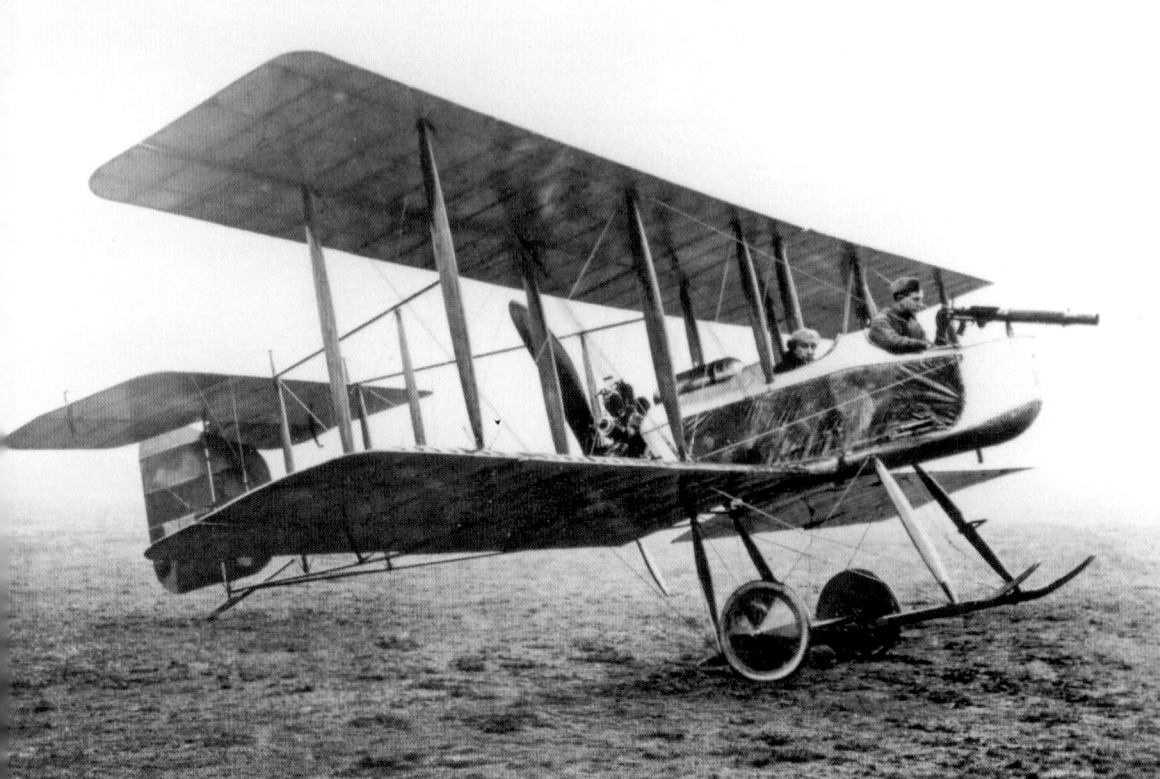

An early fighter of the Great War, the Vickers F.B.5 Gunbus. (*Flight* via Key Archives)

The Vickers F.B.5 Gunbus appeared in 1914, having had its first flight on 17 July. It was powered by a Gnome Monosoupape 100hp (75kW), giving a top speed of 70mph (112km/h). The machine was equipped with a single Vickers machine gun on a free mounting for the observer who occupied the front cockpit.

The Gunbus was constructed with spruce spars and ribs for the wings, and was fabric covered. The nacelle was a wooden structure with a plywood-covered nose and decking with fabric aft. There were wooden walkways attached to each side of the nacelle near the front cockpit. The booms carrying the tail plane and rudder were steel tubes spaced vertically by spruce struts. The F.B.5 had a wingspan of 36ft 6in (11.13m) and a length of 27ft 2in (8.28m).

The first operational F.B.5 was delivered to the RFC in November 1914 and on 25 December the first action took place when an F.B.5 attacked a Rumpler Taube, hitting the Taube and possibly causing its loss. Less than three weeks later, the same F.B.5 was forced to land behind German lines and the aircraft fell into enemy hands.

In early February 1915, the F.B.5 started to appear on the Western Front and in July of that year, the first fighter squadron was fully equipped with the aircraft. It had a British-built engine but these proved to be less reliable than the French-built version.

A total of 224 Vickers F.B.5 aircraft were built. Of this number, 56 were constructed by a French company, SA Darracq, and 12 by Danish Arsenal Workshops.

By the end of 1915, the F.B.5 aircraft was outclassed by the Fokker Eindecker with its synchronised machine gun, so it was retired in the spring of 1916 following the arrival of the Vickers F.B.9 Gunbus.

White and Thompson No.3

The White and Thompson Company of Bognor Regis in Sussex had become Great Britain licence holder for Curtiss flying boats in 1913. The *Daily Mail* newspaper sponsored a Circuit of Britain race for seaplanes with a prize of £5,000, a significant sum at that time. The race was due to start on 10 August 1914.

White and Thompson entered the competition and built a single-engined pusher aircraft called the White and Thompson No.2 Flying Boat. Construction of the hull was sub-contracted to an Isle of Wight company, S.E. Saunders Ltd. The hull was made of copper-sewn mahogany over a wooden frame. The engine was a 120hp (90kW) Austro Daimler unit built by Beardmore and it was mounted between the upper and lower wings, but clear of both. A crew of two was seated side-by-side in an open cockpit.

The No.2 flew on 1 August 1914, but given that Great Britain declared war on Germany on 4 August, the aircraft was pressed into military service by the RNAS. An order for eight more aircraft was received and these were designated White and Thompson No.3. They differed from the No.2 in the profile of the wings and a modified fin arrangement. These production aircraft were powered by a 120hp (90kW) Beardmore engine.

The original prototype was fitted with bomb racks and served with the RNAS until it was wrecked in June 1915. Production aircraft were delivered from February 1915 and were deployed on anti-submarine patrols from bases in the UK and France. A Lewis machine gun could be fitted to the side of the hull.

The production aircraft had a top speed of 85mph (137km/h). The wingspan was 45ft (13.72m) and the length was 27ft 6in (8.38m).

An artist's depiction of the White and Thompson No.3 aircraft. (Picryl)

Martinsyde S.1

The Martinsyde S.1 was developed as a fighter/scout broadly in the format of the Sopwith Tabloid and Bristol Scout. Power was supplied by an 80hp (60kW) Gnome rotary engine, which gave the aircraft a top speed of 87mph (140km/h) and a service ceiling of 14,000ft (4,267m). It was armed with a single Lewis machine gun mounted above the centre section.

The S.1 was ordered for the RFC and about 60 aircraft were constructed. It entered service in 1914 but only limited numbers saw operations in France. The S.1 was deployed in the Middle East, but in very small numbers. It was found that the rotary engine did not cope well with the climate and dust of Mesopotamia (in modern day Iraq). Even so, they were still in use in November 1915 in Libya, but the final surviving aircraft of the Middle East operation was abandoned in April 1916. Any remaining S.1s on the Western Front had been relegated to training roles in Britain.

The S.1 was also used by the Australian Flying Corps. The Martinsyde S.1 had a wingspan of 27ft 8in (8.43m) and a length of 21ft (6.4m).

A dismantled Martinsyde S.1, probably in Mesopotamia. (Picryl)

Sopwith Schneider

The Tabloid had demonstrated its performance as a single-seat scout, and as a floatplane by winning the 1914 Schneider Trophy Air Race. In 1914, the RNAS placed an order for 12 'Schneider' floatplanes. These were powered by the 100hp (75kW) Gnome Monosoupape engine and were nearly identical to the race-winning aircraft except for the design of the tail float.

Although early aircraft relied on wing-warping for lateral control, later versions were fitted with ailerons and carried a Lewis machine gun firing upwards through a wing centre section opening.

During 1915, there were attempts to use Sopwith Schneiders to intercept Zeppelins over the North Sea, probably as these were climbing towards Britain. These attempts do not appear to have been successful.

A total of about 135 Sopwith Schneiders were built. One Schneider was sold to the Imperial Japanese Navy Air Service.

It had a top speed of 87mph (140km/h), a service ceiling of 7,000ft (2,100m) and a range of 510 miles (820km). The wingspan was 25ft 8in (7.82m) and the length was 22ft 10in (6.96m).

The Sopwith Schneider floatplane. (Picryl)

Armstrong Whitworth F.K.3

In 1914, a Dutch aircraft designer, Frederick Koolhoven, joined Sir W.G. Armstrong-Whitworth Ltd of Newcastle-upon-Tyne. The aircraft he designed bore his initials.

At the time, Armstrong-Whitworth was building the Royal Aircraft Factory B.E.2c for the RFC. Koolhoven felt that he could improve on the structure of it, making it easier to build by eliminating some welds and complex structures. Seven aircraft were built, powered by an air-cooled 70hp (52kW) Renault engine. These are sometimes known as the F.K.2s.

These seven machines were rejected for frontline service in France. The design was then modified and subsequent aircraft had an air-cooled 90hp (67kW) Royal Aircraft Factory 1a engine, revisions to the fin and rudder, changes to the wing layout and a single extended cockpit accommodating the pilot and observer. This last point enabled the pilot to occupy the front seat and allowed the observer a clearer field of vision for the use of a Lewis machine gun.

Tests showed that the F.K.3 had a better performance than the B.E.2c, but could carry a smaller payload. An order for 150 aircraft was issued to Armstrong-Whitworth and another order for 350 machines to sub-contractor Hewlett & Blondeau Ltd of Luton. Construction of the F.K.3 followed conventional lines, being made of wood with fabric covering. The wingspan was 42ft 5in (12.94m) and the length was 29ft 9in (9.07m).

At one point during manufacture, there was a shortage of Royal Aircraft Factory engines and 12 aircraft were fitted with a water-cooled Beardmore engine of 120hp (89kW) instead. The additional weight required an increase of 2ft (0.61m) in the wingspan but there was no marked change in overall performance and the aircraft had the Royal Aircraft Factory engines fitted when they became available. If the aircraft was flown as a single-seat machine, it could carry a bombload of up to 112lb (51kg).

The F.K.3 had a top speed of 87mph (139km/h), a service ceiling of 12,000ft (3,658m) and an endurance of three hours. It was not used for operational purposes in France as there were more advanced and capable aircraft in prospect. A squadron based on Salonika (now Thessalonika), Greece, received F.K.3s, the remainder being used as trainers in the UK.

The Royal Australian Air Force used the Armstrong-Whitworth F.K.3 for training, and the Bulgarian Air Force captured one example in 1917, which it used.

The Armstrong Whitworth F.K.3 was mainly used for training. (*Aeroplane* via Key Archives)

Royal Aircraft Factory B.E.2c

The B.E.2c was a development of the original design, with staggered wings and other improvements in stability, which unfortunately made the controls heavy. A small variety of powerplants were initially installed, but production aircraft were fitted with a Royal Aircraft Factory 1a engine, a development of the Renault engine that delivered 90hp (67kW). It had a top speed of 72mph (115km/h) and the service ceiling was 11,000ft (3,353m).

Deliveries to squadrons began in 1915 and it continued in service until 1917, long after the aircraft had proved itself to be obsolete and not fit for operational service. Baron Manfred von Richthofen was still shooting down B.E.2 variants in late April 1917.

The B.E.2c was equipped with a variety of armaments, but because the aircraft was flown from the rear seat, the observer/gunner in the front seat had a very limited field of view. Indeed, pilots of one squadron were known to have removed a Lewis machine gun in disgust. Although some aircraft were fitted with underwing racks for carrying bombs, in practice the observer was frequently unable to fly on a bombing operation because the engine power was not sufficient to manage the additional weight of bombs.

Unfortunately, Anthony Fokker had developed an interrupter gear to enable a machine gun to fire through the propeller arc on the Fokker Eindekker fighter, making that machine an extremely formidable opponent. Much of 1915 became known as the Fokker Scourge because German air superiority proved formidable. Against this, the B.E.2c machines were effectively defenceless because their role was reconnaissance and gun-setting for the artillery, which required concentration on the ground and steady flying.

Although the inherent stability of the B.E.2c made it an excellent flying machine, its inability to take effective evasive action when attacked added to its unpopularity among aircrew. Unfortunately, it had been selected for large-scale production and those with the power to withdraw the aircraft chose to select quantity over quality. The result was that the B.E.2c was retained for two years longer than it should have been. At the end of the Great War, the B.E.2c and B.E.2d aircraft were still in service with Home Defence units and with training units in Great Britain, Egypt, Palestine, Salonika and East Africa.

Its construction was conventional wood with fabric covering; its wingspan was 37ft (11.28m) and its length was 27ft 3in (8.31m). The fuel tank held 26 imperial gallons (117 litres/31 US gallons) of petrol.

The Royal Aircraft Factory B.E.2c; defenceless and obsolete, but still issued to squadrons. (Picryl)

Royal Aircraft Factory B.E.2d

The B.E.2d was essentially a B.E.2c fitted with dual controls. In order for controls to be fitted in the front cockpit, normally the observer's position, the fuel tank had to be removed. The fuel tank, which was formerly situated under the observer's seat, was replaced with a gravity tank fitted on the upper wing centre section. This was a large tank needed for endurance, but it increased drag which reduced performance. Most B.E.2ds were used as trainers.

The B.E.2ds supplied to the Belgian Air Force were fitted with Hispano engines and some had the pilot's and observer's seats reversed, giving the observer a much better field of fire.

The B.E.2d ready for take-off in a desert location. (Picryl)

A Belgian Army B.E.2d with the Hispano engine. (Public domain, via Wikimedia Commons)

Wight Pusher Seaplane

In early 1914, John Samuel White & Company Ltd (Wight Aircraft), based in East Cowes on the Isle of Wight, designed and built a two-seat seaplane. It was a pusher aircraft, powered by a single 200hp (149kW) Salmson Canton Unne water-cooled radial engine. It had a wingspan of 63ft (19.2m). The aircraft had a top speed of 72mph (115km/h), a service ceiling of 9,600ft (2,926m) and a six-hour endurance. It was known as the Wight Pusher Seaplane, but also simply as the Navyplane.

The company had a long history in the marine industry and had been shipbuilders since the 17th century. For a period up until 1913, the company employed an apprentice, Barnes Wallis, who may have had a hand in the original design of the Wight Pusher. Barnes Wallis later joined Vickers as an aircraft designer, becoming famous for his geodetic construction of aircraft such as the Wellington bomber and, of course, the 'bouncing bomb' dropped by the 'Dambusters' in May 1943.

The first Wight Pusher aircraft was exhibited at the Olympia Air Show, West London, in March 1914, with the first flight taking place on 8 April. Its performance was impressive with take-off, climb and endurance being particularly strong points. As a result, the RNAS ordered three aircraft, and the German navy (Kaiserliche Marine) ordered four. One of these machines was delivered, but it then became apparent that war might break out and White refused to deliver the remaining aircraft, which were taken over by the RNAS for anti-submarine patrols.

Orders for seven more aircraft, designated Improved Navyplane Type A.I, were issued. These aircraft had stronger airframes, folding wings and an increased wingspan of 8ft (2.4m). These aircraft continued with the Salmson engine. An additional four aircraft, designated Improved Navyplane Type A.II, were built fitted with 225hp (168kW) Sunbeam engines.

The Navyplanes were deployed on maritime reconnaissance activities over the North Sea, but four of the Improved Navyplane Type I machines were shipped to the Dardenelles to serve in the Gallipoli Campaign. Meanwhile, the Sunbeam engines had proved unreliable and those aircraft saw limited use.

The Wight Pusher Seaplane. (Alamy)

White and Thompson N.T.3 'Bognor Bloater'

White and Thompson Ltd were based at Middleton-on-Sea, a suburb of Bognor Regis, West Sussex. What became known as the Bognor Bloater was designed as a competitor to the Royal Aircraft Factory B.E.2. It was unusual in having a monocoque fuselage, with the weight of the aircraft being supported by the external skin; in the case of the Bognor Bloater it was a cedar skin sewn together with copper. It was the first aircraft to employ such a technique and this may have been the source of the aircraft's name.

Power came from a 70hp (52kW) Renault in-line engine. It was a much better looking aircraft than its nickname implied. Its wingspan was 37ft (11.28m) and its length was 28ft 3in (8.61m).

The Bloater's first flight was in March 1915 and the RNAS ordered 12 aircraft, but only ten were delivered, the remaining two being retained as spares. The Bloater had a crew of two. It was used in a limited capacity as a communications and training machine and for coastal patrols from stations at Eastbourne, Great Yarmouth and Killingholme. In 1916, it was withdrawn from service.

The Bognor Bloater on the beach at or near Bognor Regis in Sussex. (Roger Staker, from the late aviation historian John McIntosh Bruce)

Bristol Scout

The Bristol Scout was designed in 1913 as a racing aircraft, and first flew on 23 February 1914. It handled well and had a good performance from an 80hp (60kW) Gnome engine. Even so, some modifications were made, including increasing both the chord and span of the wings, a larger rudder and new cowling. In March 1914, it was exhibited at the Olympia Aero Show in London.

In May, the Scout was evaluated at Farnborough by military personnel. Bristol's chief test pilot managed to achieve a speed of 97.5mph (157km/h). So impressive was this performance that the aircraft was entered in a number of air races, but a variety of mishaps robbed it of victory. In July 1914, it was entered in a London–Paris–London race, but on the return leg it ran out of fuel and was ditched in the English Channel. The pilot was rescued but the aircraft was lost. The cause was failure to fill both of the two fuel tanks! This one-off aircraft became known as the Scout A.

The next two aircraft were requestioned by the War Office shortly after the outbreak of war. These were designated Scout B and differed from the original in having an enlarged rudder and other relatively minor changes.

The War Office was impressed and in November 1914 an order for 12 aircraft for the RFC was placed, and the RNAS ordered 24 more. This was the first production model of the Scout 'C'. The 36 aircraft ordered were followed by a further 125, 50 for the RNAS and 75 for the RFC. They were powered by 80hp (60kW) Gnome, Le Rhone or Clerget engines.

The Bristol Scout was widely used in the early part of 1915. Strangely, by modern standards, they were issued only in ones and twos to squadrons so that no squadron had a full complement of a single type of aircraft. On 25 July 1915, Captain Lance Hawker shot down two German aircraft and forced a third to retreat over Passchendaele and Zillebeke in Flanders, using a Martini Carbine mounted on his Scout C. For this action he was awarded the Victoria Cross.

The Bristol Scout was popular with pilots and high-ranking officers. (Roger Staker)

Like other British aircraft, at this stage of the war, the Scouts that were initially delivered had no armament. They were viewed as being simply faster reconnaissance equipment. However, this changed when an early type of interrupter gear was fitted allowing a Vickers machine gun to be mounted firing through the propeller arc. At this point, its main purpose was changed to acting as an escort fighter for the two-seat reconnaissance aircraft, which still formed the majority of RFC and RNAS machines.

As with many aircraft of the period, the Bristol Scout saw a number of variations to the basic design either as a result of operational feedback or changes to the powerplant choice. The most numerous version was the Scout 'D'. In total, 210 were built with 130 going to the RFC, and the remainder to the RNAS.

Powerplants fitted included the 80hp (60kW) Gnome or Le Rhone rotary engines, the 100hp (75kW) Monosoupape rotary engine, or the 105hp (78kW) Le Rhone rotary engine. The 80hp (60kW) engines gave a maximum speed of 89mph (142km/h), rising to 104mph (166km/h) for the 100hp (75kW) Monosoupape. Its wingspan was 24ft 7in (7.48m) and its length was 20ft 8in (6.3m). The construction followed the common approach of a wooden framework with a fabric covering.

The Scout 'D' had excellent flying and handling characteristics, making it popular among pilots, and particularly high-ranking officers, who used them as private 'mounts'. At least 80 Scout 'D's saw service in France and 32 were deployed to squadrons in the Middle East. Bristol Scouts were also used by the Australian Air Force and the Hellenic Navy. The Ottoman Air Force used captured Scouts. The last Bristol Scout in service is believed to have been a former RNAS Scout D of the Australian Air Force, which was still in use in October 1926.

Had this aircraft been available earlier in the war and with the interrupter mechanism to provide synchronisation between the propeller and the machine gun, it would have been one of the finest – possibly the best – aircraft operated by any nation.

The internal structure of the Bristol Scout is fully on view. (Roger Staker)

Wight 840

In 1914, the Wight Company saw the opportunity to use the 225hp (168kW) Sunbeam water-cooled engine to power a new float plane. The design was a two-seat floatplane, with twin floats of sufficient length to obviate the need for a tail float.

The company had already demonstrated its ability to produce float planes with good performance and the Type 840 was designed to carry the Whitehead Mk.IX 14in (0.36m) torpedo. The Wight 840 had a wingspan of 61ft (18.59m) and a length of 41ft (12.5m). As an alternative to the torpedo, the 840 could carry up to 810lb (367kg) of bombs.

Short Bros was also developing a very similar aircraft, the Short S.184. The main obvious difference between the two machines was the need for a tail float on the S.184. Although the S.184 was probably the better aircraft, the RNAS nevertheless ordered 68 Wight 840s. In the event, 52 were fully built and delivered and a number, perhaps as many as 18, were constructed but retained as spares.

The Wight aircraft did not see any frontline service but was employed on coastal anti-submarine patrols operating from British naval bases at Felixstowe and Scapa Flow and also Gibraltar. By 1917, it had been retired.

The Sunbeam motor gave the aircraft a top speed of just over 80mph (128km/h) without the torpedo, and an endurance of seven hours.

A Wight 840 anti-submarine aircraft. (Johan Visschenijk, 1000aircraftphotos.com)

Sopwith Baby

In 1915, the Sopwith Baby appeared. This was a seaplane designed for the RNAS, a development of the Sopwith Schneider and as a direct result of the success of the Tabloid Scout. Unlike the Tabloid, the Baby had its rotary powerplant only partially shielded by a cowling. Engines fitted during its service life were a 100hp Gnome Monosoupape, a 110hp (82kW) Clerget or a 130hp (97kW) Clerget. The Baby had a top speed of 98mph (157km/h) and an endurance of two hours.

The construction was a wood and fabric covering. With a wingspan of only 25ft 8in (7.82m) and a length of 22ft 10in (6.96m), the Baby lived up to its name. The RNAS ordered 286 Sopwith Baby aircraft, 100 being built by Sopwith and the remainder mainly by Blackburn Aircraft at Leeds. Another 100 aircraft were built under licence by SA Aeronautica Gio Ansaldo in Turin, Italy, for the Italian Navy.

The Baby was fitted with three floats, the two fitted to the wings protruding beyond the engine nacelle and the third fitted under the fin and rudder assembly. As the power increased with the more powerful engines, so did the work the Baby was expected to do. The aircraft was fitted with a Lewis machine gun mounted to fire at an angle upwards through the cut-out in the upper wing centre section. It was later fitted with bomb racks for two 65lb (29.5kg) bombs but frequently flew with two machine guns, 130lb (59kg) of bombs, a carrier pigeon, fresh water supplies and a sea anchor. The overloading of the Baby caused concern for pilots and the aircraft fell into disrepute, but this was eventually resolved when the 130hp (97kW) engine version appeared.

The Sopwith Baby was used as a shipborne reconnaissance aircraft and bomber, and was operated from cruisers and other craft, being hoisted into and from the sea when required. The RNAS based them at coastal air stations as well as at RNAS stations in Egypt, Greece and Italy.

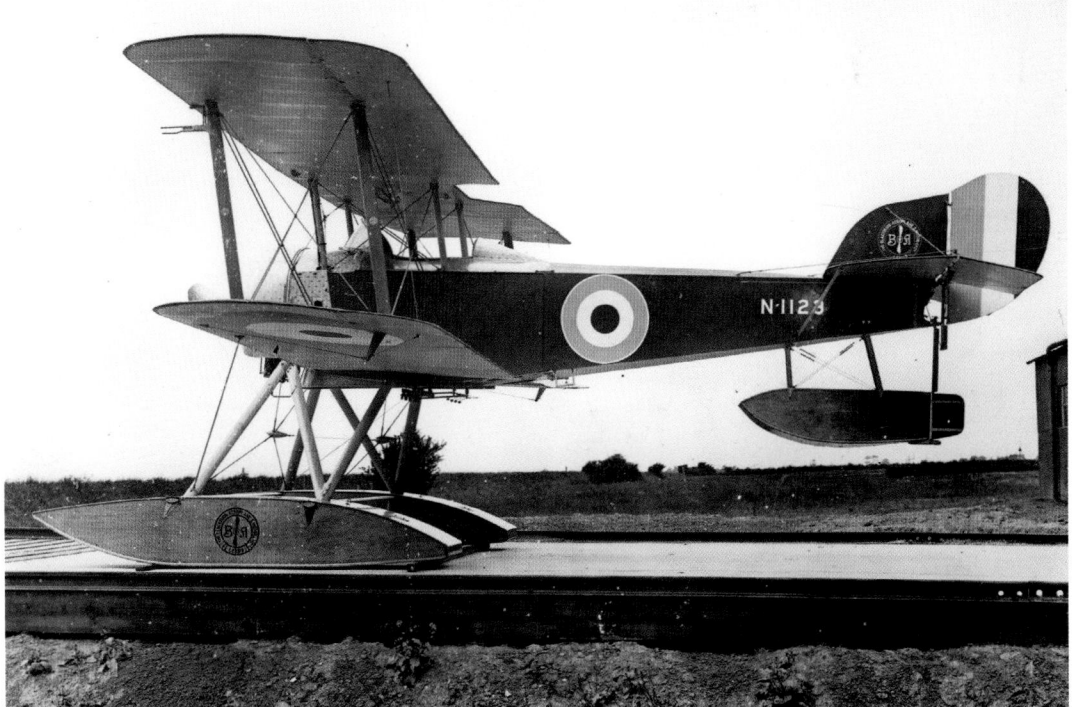

The Sopwith Baby was a descendant of the Schneider Trophy-winning aircraft. (Blackburn and General Aircraft Ltd via *Flight* via Key Archives)

In addition to the RNAS, the Baby was operated by the air forces of Australia, France, Greece, Italy, Japan, Norway and the US. An RNAS Baby was forced to land off the Dutch coast and was towed into a Dutch port and interned. After the war, the Chilean Navy operated a few Sopwith Baby aircraft until 1923. In June 1928, two of the Royal Norwegian Navy Sopwith Baby floatplanes were deployed in the search for Roald Amundsen, the polar explorer, who had disappeared, but it is not thought that the aircraft were used. Amundsen's body was never found.

By October 1918, there were 59 Baby aircraft serving with RNAS stations around Britain and also in Belgium.

Fairey Aviation was building Sopwith Baby floatplanes as a sub-contractor. In late October 1916, a Sopwith Baby was sent to Fairey Aviation for repair. Rather than carry out the repair, Fairey took the opportunity to rebuild it and incorporate some of its own innovations. The most significant modification was to install the Fairey Patent Camber Gear. This was a form of flap along the entire trailing edge of both wings. They were hinged on the main spar and operated by rotation of a handwheel in the cockpit. Lowered flaps increased lift and doubtless reduced the landing speed. A device ensured that the flaps could also be operated conventionally as ailerons, ensuring lateral control was not detrimentally affected.

Compared with the Sopwith Baby, the 'Fairey' aircraft had wings with increased span but reduced chord, with rounded wing tips. The tailplane was changed in shape and the floats were modified, with a larger tail float. About 180 Fairey Hamble Baby aircraft were built. In addition to the RAF, the Hamble Baby was used by the Hellenic Navy.

Fitted with a 110hp (82kW) Clerget rotary engine, the Hamble Baby had a maximum speed of 92mph (148km/h) and a service ceiling of 7,500ft (2,300m). Its wingspan was 27ft 9¼in (8.46m) and its length was 23ft 4in (7.11m).

A Sopwith Baby awaiting restoration at the Yeovilton Fleet Air Arm Museum.

Short '225' Seaplane Type S.184

Short Bros, based in Kent, was responsible for a variety of successful seaplanes that saw service with the RNAS. The name '225' actually derived from the 225hp (168kW) Sunbeam Mohawk motor of the first 1915 version of the seaplane and became the generic name for all subsequent versions. On the assurance of Horace Short that the company could design and build a seaplane to meet the needs of the Admiralty, two prototypes were ordered. These were given the serial numbers 184 and 185, hence the 'Type S.184' name.

Like the Sopwith Baby, the Short Type S.184 had triple floats with the third sitting under the fin. This tail float featured a small water rudder operated by torque from the main 'air' rudder. The fuselage and wings were wooden with fabric covering and manganese steel fittings, but the floats were mahogany structures with steel supports with wooden fairings. The wingspan was 63ft 6½in (19.36m) and it was 40ft 7in (12.36m) long. The wings folded for handling and storage.

The first prototype flew early in 1915. Initial trials indicated a lack of longitudinal control and the ailerons, fitted only to the upper wings and reliant on airflow to return them to the neutral position, were a source of problems when taxiing downwind. Ailerons were fitted to the lower wings of all subsequent aircraft and controlled by cables linking the upper and lower ailerons and had bungee cords to return them to the neutral position.

An order for ten aircraft had already been placed, and a total of 936 Short Type 184 seaplanes were eventually built, constructed by ten British aircraft manufacturers. These later versions were fitted with either the 240hp (179kW) Renault-Mercedes motor or the 260hp (194kW) Sunbeam. A radio transmitter and receiver were installed with power provided by a wind-driven generator, which could be folded away

A Short '225' Seaplane Type S.184; a successful aircraft with an interesting story. (Picryl)

when not in use. A basket of carrier pigeons was included as standard equipment, a common form of emergency communication.

On 21 March 1915, the two prototypes embarked on HMS *Ben-my-Chree*, a Royal Navy packet steamer and seaplane carrier, bound for the Aegean to provide support for the Gallipoli campaign. On 12 August 1915, one of these Type 184s became the first aircraft in the world to attack an enemy ship with a torpedo launched from the air. This ship had already been attacked by a British submarine, but on 17 August, a Turkish transport ship was sunk by a torpedo launched by one of the seaplanes.

By a strange twist of fate, the accompanying Type 184 was forced to land on the sea because of engine trouble but the crew spotted an enemy tug. It managed to taxi up to it and release the aircraft's torpedo causing the tug to sink. Now relieved of the torpedo's weight, the crew managed to take off and return to its seaplane carrier.

Designed as a two-seat observation and torpedo bomber aircraft, a Type S.184 was involved in reconnaissance flights over German warships at the Battle of Jutland, which took place on 31 May–1 June 1916 off the coast of Denmark. This gave the aircraft the distinction of being the only British aircraft to be involved in a naval sea battle during the Great War.

The Short Type S.184 had a top speed of 84mph (134km/h). Armament was a single Lewis machine gun ring-mounted in the rear cockpit. It could carry either a torpedo or 400lb (182kg) of bombs. A later model could carry four 112lb (51kg) bombs. A single seat derivative, the 'D', held nine 56lb (25.45kg) bombs vertically in front of the pilot's cockpit. A Turkish transport ship was sunk at sea by a torpedo dropped from a Type S.184.

More than 300 Short Type S.184 seaplanes had been delivered to the RNAS by the time the Armistice was signed in November 1918, and they were still in production. They were mainly deployed on anti-submarine and convoy protection duties, operating from the East Coast of Britain but a small number also served in Mesopotamia. They proved to be rugged, reliable and very seaworthy, making them ideal for the conditions in which they were required to operate.

The Type 184 remained in RNAS service until the early 1920s, but all were struck off charge in 1922 as part of the drive to reduce government expenditure. Other users of the Short Type 184 included the Canadian Naval Air Service, Chilean Air Force and Chilean Navy (which operated them until 1933), Estonian Air Force (also operating them until 1933), French Navy, Hellenic Navy, Imperial Japanese Navy and the Dutch Naval Aviation Service.

Airco DH1A

The DH1 was a product of the Aircraft Manufacturing Company (Airco). The chief designer, Geoffrey de Havilland, used his design skills to tackle the problem of operating fighting aircraft while avoiding shooting down your own machine's propeller via the DH1. He was not alone in this. It is significant not so much for its achievements in operation, but more for the fact that this was the first of a long line of very successful aircraft bearing the design skills of Geoffrey de Havilland. The DH1 was intended as a two-seat fighter/reconnaissance aircraft.

Although designed for a Beardmore engine, delivery delays meant that the DH1 prototype was powered by a 70hp (52kW) Renault air-cooled engine. With this motor, the aircraft was underpowered, but performance was still enough to secure an order for 49 machines. When supplies of the 120hp (89kW) Beardmore engine became available, the later aircraft were fitted with the intended engine. These aircraft were designated DH1A and an additional order for 50 aircraft was placed.

Because the Aircraft Manufacturing Company was heavily committed to the design and manufacture of other aircraft, the construction of the DH1 and DH1A was sub-contracted to Savages Ltd of King's Lynn. It is an interesting commentary on the construction of early biplanes that Savages had been a manufacturer of fairground equipment. The wings were a wooden framework with fabric covering. The nacelle was a wooden structure with fabric and plywood covering. The wingspan was 41ft 4in (12.6m), and the length was 29ft 3in (8.92m).

Despite the first flight having taken place in January 1915, production proved to be very slow and by the end of 1915 only five aircraft had been delivered to the RFC.

Early deliveries to operational squadrons were limited by production difficulties with the 120hp (89kW) Beardmore engine. This gave the aircraft a maximum speed of 90mph (144km/h). The DH1A was a two-seat pusher design, with the observer situated in the front cockpit having the use of a Lewis machine gun. Its role was both as a reconnaissance aircraft and also, but probably secondary, as a fighter. In reality, it was already bordering on obsolescence and was soon replaced by single-seat scouts.

A total of 100 DH1s were constructed. The aircraft saw service on the Home Defence Front, as escorts for B.E.2 aircraft on the Western Front and a few in the Middle East. In August 1916, a DH1A shot down a German two-seater Aviatik, the only recorded victory by the type. By 1917, DH1s had been withdrawn from service.

The Airco DH1A fighter. (Picryl)

Airco DH2

More significant than the DH1A was its successor, the DH2. This was intended as a fighter-scout. Design started before the 1915 'Fokker Scourge' resulting from Anthony Fokker's brilliant invention of the machine gun interrupter gear fitted to the Fokker Eindekker. This avoided the need for either a pilot or observer to use a flexible and often awkwardly mounted machine gun at an angle to the flying direction of the aircraft, effectively meaning instantaneous decisions being made on angles of deflection. With the Eindekker, the pilot had simply to point his aircraft at the opponent. Nevertheless, the timing of the DH2s arrival on the Western Front was advantageous.

Operational experience with the DH1 showed that a single-seat fighter was needed, rather than the relatively lumbering two-seater pusher aircraft. The DH2 was a scaled down version of the DH1 in many respects, and was effectively designed around the Lewis machine gun, which it carried on a free mounting in front of the pilot. Later, the gun became fixed when it was realised that the most accurate way of aiming at the enemy was to point the aircraft itself in the direction of the target. Construction was the same as the DH1A, a wooden framework with fabric covering. Its wingspan was 28ft 3in (8.61m) and its length 25ft 3in (7.69m).

The first prototype flew in July 1915 and after the standard manufacturer's trials, it was despatched to France for evaluation. Unfortunately, it was shot down over the Western Front with the loss of the pilot. The aircraft fell into German hands and was repaired. Even so, the DH2 was ordered into production with deliveries to the RFC commencing in the second half of 1915, and by the end of that year a small number were operational in France.

The DH2 was powered by a Gnome Monosoupape rotary engine of 100hp (75kW) giving a top speed of 86mph (138k/h). Some later models were fitted with a 110hp (82kW) Le Rhone engine, which increased

The Airco DH2 fighter saw service until 1917. (via Key Archives)

the top speed to 93mph (150km/h). Aerodynamic efficiency was not the DH2's best characteristic, a result of the pusher layout, with performance suffering as a result, but it still proved a match to the Fokker when it was introduced to frontline service in late 1915 and early 1916. It became the first British aircraft to fully equip a squadron with a single type.

It seems that the first DH2 victory over a Fokker Eindekker probably occurred on 2 April 1916. Indeed, the DH2 helped British forces achieve supremacy in the air during 1916, a key element during the Battle of the Somme between 1 July and mid-November 1916. By the end of that year, more than 220 DH2s were in France and more than 450 were produced before it was overtaken by the manufacture of later aircraft. Even so, it was still in service until mid-1917.

Pilot James McCudden became an 'ace' flying the DH2 and, later, the S.E.5A.

The DH2 was an interim answer to the Fokker Scourge. (Picryl, public domain)

Royal Aircraft Factory R.E.5

The R.E.5 was a product of the Royal Aircraft Factory and was designed for reconnaissance and artillery observation, but it was also deployed as a day bomber. It was a two-seat conventional aircraft; the wings were constructed with a wooden framework and covered in fabric while the fuselage was in part constructed with steel tubing, again fabric covered.

Because the R.E.5 was considered to be a development of existing Royal Aircraft Factory aircraft rather than a new design, there was no prototype. It was ordered into production in late 1913 and the first production aircraft flew on 26 January 1914. During the first two weeks of February, the second, third and fourth R.E.5s also had their first flights, such was the rate of production.

The R.E.5 was powered by an Austro-Daimler engine of 120hp (89kW), or its equivalent, built by Beardmore in the UK, giving the aircraft a maximum speed of 79mph (126km/h). With a wingspan of 45ft 3in (13.8m) it was a large aircraft.

A total of 24 R.E.5 aircraft were built, a relatively large order for the time. About half of these served in France during the summer of 1915, with the remainder serving with training units. The R.E.5 has been described as being a wholly indifferent aircraft and surprisingly little seems to be known about its operational history.

The Royal Aircraft Factory R.E.5. (via Key Archives)

Short Type 827

Built as a two-seat reconnaissance floatplane, the Short 827 was a slightly smaller version of the Short 166 floatplane, a reconnaissance, bomber and torpedo-carrying floatplane designed to operate from HMS *Ark Royal*. A total of 26 were built, mainly by sub-contractors.

Production of the Type 827 began in April 1914. Shortages of the preferred Salmson engines meant that the first eight aircraft were fitted with 100hp (75kW) Gnome Monosoupape engines. The next batch of six had 135hp (101kW) Salmson engines, but by then the new 150hp (112kW) Sunbeam Nubian water-cooled engine had become available. The Type 827 was modified to accept the new engine. As a result, the speed increased by 9mph (15km/h).

To ensure adequate cooling, a radiator system was fitted above the engine, consisting of spiral tubes assembled into a block providing excellent cooling as hot water would naturally rise to the top, reducing the reliance on a water pump. Although this feature looked clumsy and reduced the pilot's view, it was not as serious as it appeared and there were benefits for the crew because they received a stream of warm air. The radiator remained a feature of later Short seaplanes.

Trials on HMS *Campania* proved satisfactory and production orders were placed with Short Brothers and sub-contractors including the Sunbeam Motor Company, Parnall & Sons and Brush Electrical Engineering as well as Fairey Aviation Company. By 1915, the Type 827 was becoming the standard RNAS equipment.

When German battleships shelled the east coast towns of Yarmouth, Southwold and Lowestoft in April 1915, RNAS aircraft, including a Type 827 seaplane, bombed the German ships. As well as Home Defence operations, Type 827s served in the Mediterranean and in several African operations, where performance was limited by the climate.

In addition to 108 Type 827s, a variant with a 135hp (101kW) Salmson water-cooled engine was built and designated the Type 830. Only eight Type 830s were constructed. The Type 827 and Type 830 continued in service until October 1918, although in reducing numbers and in secondary roles.

The Type 827 with the Sunbeam Nubian engine had a top speed of 62mph (100km/h) and an endurance of three hours 30 minutes. The Type 830's top speed was 70mph (113km/h). The wingspan of both types was 53ft 11in (16.43m) and the length was 35ft 3in (10.74m). Armament was a single Lewis machine gun on a flexible mount in the rear cockpit, with the ability to carry light bombs under the wings.

A Short Type 827 showing its large cooling system, which helped keep the crew warm. (Picryl)

Sopwith 860

The relatively crude structure of the seaplanes available in 1914, and particularly the low power of their engines, greatly limited the potential for torpedo-carrying aircraft to undertake operational missions. For many aircraft, the power simply was insufficient to lift the aircraft and torpedo out of the water. Sopwith persevered and decided that the solution was to build a seaplane of modest dimensions and equip it with the most powerful engine then available, the 225hp (168kW) Sunbeam Mohawk. The RNAS was impressed and although no prototype was ordered, a production order for 22 aircraft was placed in the autumn of 1914.

By early 1915, 18 aircraft, designated the Sopwith 860, had been built. On 27 January 1915, the first flight with a torpedo took place. The pilot occupied the rear cockpit, with the observer in the front under the upper wing centre section through which a large cut-out provided visibility. Logically a machine gun could have been provided, but this does not seem to have been the case. The wings folded for storage and handling.

Although the Sopwith 860 remained in service until at least 1916, it does not seem to have been engaged in any action of distinction. Apart from the wingspan of 62ft 11in (19.18m), very little is known about the aircraft.

The Sopwith 860. (Alamy)

Sopwith Type 807

In 1914, the *Daily Mail* newspaper staged an air race called the Circuit of Britain race for seaplanes. Sopwith built a tractor biplane powered by an 100hp (75kW) Gnome Monosoupape rotary engine for the competition. On 16 July 1914, it had its first flight, but as a landplane. It was then fitted with its floats.

The outbreak of war in August meant the cancellation of the race, but the Circuit of Britain aircraft were purchased by the Admiralty. A version of Sopwith's aircraft was ordered into production by the Admiralty, becoming designated as the Type 807. The upper wingspan was increased and the wings were adapted to fold using a mechanism invented by Short Brothers. Tandem cockpits were fitted with the observer sitting in the front under the leading edge of the upper wing, and the pilot under the trailing edge of the same.

The original Circuit of Britain aircraft was used by the Royal Navy. When its floats were damaged in September 1914 it was refitted with a land undercarriage. It was employed as a trainer until 22 June 1915.

Twelve Type 807s were ordered by the RNAS. In February 1915, three of these embarked for the Dardanelles on board HMS *Ark Royal*, a seaplane carrier, and participated in the Gallipoli Campaign as reconnaissance aircraft. In operations they were considered under-powered and the floats were fragile.

Although the Type 807 was unarmed, it could carry up to six small bombs. It had a maximum speed of 80mph (130km/h). Its wingspan was 43ft 6in (13.26m) and its length was 30ft 9in (9.37m).

The Sopwith Type 807 was deployed in the Gallipoli Campaign. (Dan Shumaker Collection, 1000aircraftphotos.com)

Royal Aircraft Factory B.E.2e

In 1916, the B.E.2e appeared, just in time for the Battle of the Somme, which started on 1 July of that year. It differed from the earlier B.E.2c and B.E.2d in having higher aspect ratio wings, which were intended to improve performance, and an extension in the upper wingspan by 3ft 9in (1.14m). The powerplant was a 90hp (67kW) Royal Aircraft Factory 1a, giving a top speed of 82mph (131km/h), a service ceiling of 11,000ft (3,353m) and an endurance of three hours 15 minutes. Sadly, the intention had been to equip the B.E.2c with a revised and uprated engine, the R.A.F.1b, but it had not achieved production status so the performance improvement expected over earlier models did not happen.

Like its predecessors, it was constructed of wood with a fabric covering. The upper wingspan was 40ft 9in (12.42m) and the lower wing span was 30ft 6in (9.3m).

The aircraft never became popular with aircrew. Some claimed that the upper wing extension caused flutter, others claimed it was prone to collapse. The stories were probably unfounded, but nevertheless the prejudice against the B.E.2e remained. In spring 1917, the technological balance was again swinging in Germany's favour with the introduction of the Albatros D.III, but by mid-1917, the B.E.2e was starting to be replaced by more capable aircraft.

More of this version of the B.E.2 were built than any other. In October 1918, 1,801 were in service, of which about half were in training establishments.

The Royal Aircraft Factory B.E.2e was the most numerous version of the B.E. series of aircraft. (Johan Visschedijk, 1000aircraftphotos.com)

Vickers F.B.9 Gunbus

The Vickers F.B.9 Gunbus was a modification of the slightly earlier F.B.5. It featured changes designed to reduce drag by 'cleaning up' the nacelle with a pointed rather than a stub nose, streamlined wires and changes to the undercarriage. It also had rounded wing tips. The prototype first flew in December 1915, powered by a 100hp (75kW) Gnome Monosoupape rotary engine. It appeared over the Western Front early in 1916.

The F.B.9 carried a single fixed forward-firing Vickers machine gun in the front cockpit, the pilot sitting in the second cockpit. It had a top speed of 82mph (131km/h), a service ceiling of 11,000ft (3,353m) and a range of 360 miles (576km).

The F.B.9's wingspan was 33ft 10in (10.33m) and its length 27ft 10in (8.51m). A total of 120 F.B.9s were built for the RFC and gave good service, eventually being replaced by the more modern and faster tractor biplanes, such as the Sopwith Pup. All Gunbus aircraft were relegated to training functions in early 1917.

A Vickers F.B.9 Gunbus. (Picryl)

Pemberton-Billing (later Supermarine) P.B.25

Another single-seat pusher fighter/scout appearing in 1915 was the Pemberton-Billing P.B.25, designed and built by Pemberton-Billing Ltd. The business was based on the River Itchen near Woolston, Southampton. Noel Pemberton-Billing set up his company in 1913 as a producer of sea-going aircraft. The first scout produced was known as the P.B.23, powered by an 80hp (60kW) Le Rhone engine operating in pusher mode. It first flew in September 1915, but failed to attract any orders.

However, an improved version was constructed, the P.B.25. This had a more powerful engine, the 100hp (75kW) Gnome Monosoupape B.2 rotary engine. It gave a top speed of 99mph (158km/h) and a range of about 200 miles (320km). In addition, changes were made to the wings, undercarriage and to the fuselage nacelle, which was covered with canvas. The wings were swept back by 11 degrees. The P.B.25 was armed with a fixed forward-firing Lewis machine gun.

The P.B.25 was 24ft 1in (7.34m) long and had a wingspan of 33ft (10.06m).

The RNAS ordered 20 aircraft, the last being delivered in February 1917. They were based at RNAS Hendon and RNAS Hornchurch. Unfortunately, the P.B.25 was not popular with pilots, acquiring a reputation for poor performance and, even worse, for being hazardous when taking off or landing. Given the rapid developments in fighter aircraft with tractor layout, by 1917 it was also viewed as an anachronism. It is not thought that it was ever used operationally and therefore performed mainly training functions.

When Noel Pemberton-Billing became an MP in 1916, he sold his company to his factory manager, Hubert Scott-Paine, who renamed the company Supermarine Aviation Works.

The unpopular Pemberton-Billing P.B.25. (Alamy)

Royal Aircraft Factory F.E.2

The original F.E.2 was designed by Geoffrey de Havilland in 1911 at the Royal Aircraft Factory. The second aircraft of 1913 was a more modern redesign with wings from the B.E.2 and utilising wing-warping for lateral control. In mid-1914, yet another redesign took place resulting in the F.E.2A, which had its first flight on 26 January 1915. It was fitted with a Green E.6 engine but it proved underpowered and so was re-equipped with the Beardmore motor. An initial order for 12 F.E.2As was placed. This version was quickly followed by the definitive F.E.2B.

The F.E.2B was a product of the Royal Aircraft Factory but a number of sub-contractors were involved, including G. & J. Weir Ltd of Glasgow, Coventry Ordnance Works, Austin, Daimler, Armstrong-Whitworth, Napier and Siddeley-Deasy, as well as Handley Page Ltd and the Blackburn Aircraft Company. Its wings were a wooden framework with a fabric covering, but the nacelle was a plywood-covered wooden structure. The tail booms were wood with wire bracing. The wingspan was 47ft 9in (14.55m), and the length was 32ft 3in (9.83m).

Initial models were fitted with a 120hp (89kW) Beardmore engine giving a top speed of only 73mph (117km/h). Later models were equipped again with Beardmore engines, but of 160hp (119kW). Even so, top speed increased only slightly to 76mph (122km/h). However, endurance was more than three hours, making it suitable for extended bombing operations.

A number of armament arrangements were tried and employed, sometimes enhanced at squadron level. However, the general arrangement was a complement of up to four Lewis machine guns, all on free-moving pivots. The observer in the front cockpit had a single Lewis on a bracket attached to the front of the fuselage nacelle. In addition, the observer had a second Lewis on a mounting between the front and rear cockpits, used for firing upward and backward over the top wing, but to operate it the luckless observer had to stand with his feet on the nacelle. The pilot had a single Lewis for forward firing, and another on a mounting above the wing centre section for rearward defence firing.

The F.E.2B arrived on the Western Front at the beginning of 1916. Although initially envisaged and used as a two-seat fighter and reconnaissance aircraft, a role in which it had some success in helping establish air supremacy up to the Battle of the Somme, it became rapidly outclassed, and by early 1917

The Royal Aircraft Factory F.E.2B, an important fighter during the Battle of the Somme. (Picryl)

it was deployed as a night bomber. It was used in this role until the end of the war. The night-flying qualities also made it useful as a Home Defence aircraft for anti-Zeppelin patrols.

F.E.2Bs were involved in the demise of some famous German aviators. In a skirmish with Fokker monoplanes near the town of Arras in France, an F.E.2B shot the wings off the machine flown by Max Immelmann, inventor of the 'Immelmann turn' which was a half-roll off the top of a loop. Near Bapaume during an engagement with German Albatros D.1s Oswald van Boelke was killed when he was in collision with another aircraft. Boelke was a mentor of Manfred von Richthofen.

A total of 1,612 F.E.2 aircraft were built. The F.E.2B was the main production model. The F.E.2C was an experimental night-fighter version in which the seating arrangements for the observer and pilot were reversed to give the pilot a better view for night landings.

An F.E.2b, almost in silhouette. (Picryl)

Royal Aircraft Factory F.E.2D

The F.E.2D was introduced during the summer of 1916 as a higher-powered version of the F.E.2B. It had a 230hp (172kW) Rolls-Royce motor, giving the aircraft a maximum speed of 93mph (149km/h) and a service ceiling of 16,500ft (5,029m) with a three-hour endurance. This was a 20mph (32km/h) advantage over the F.E.2B and a ceiling increase of 5,000ft (1,524m).

Unfortunately, the first example of the F.E.2D to be sent to France, on 30 June 1916, lost its way over the English Channel and landed behind German lines. The benefit of surprise was therefore lost. Even so, the F.E.2D was extremely manoeuvrable for a pusher type. One machine was actually looped.

The Royal Aircraft Factory F.E.2D. (Picryl)

The F.E.2D gunner's role demanded a sense of balance in the air. (Picryl)

Armament was much the same as for the F.E.2B except that there was a fixed gun on the port side of the nacelle and some aircraft had twin guns, one on each side of the nacelle. The F.E.2D suffered the same shortcoming as all other pusher fighters in that they were very vulnerable when attacked from the rear and below. To counter this, F.E.2D pilots devised a strategy whereby they formed a defensive circle and flew in a circular motion. German fighters found them almost unbeatable in such a formation and concentrated fire from the F.E.2Ds was withering. However, it meant that the British aircraft could not continue with its reconnaissance work.

There was disquiet expressed that the excellent Rolls-Royce engines were being 'wasted' on a virtually obsolete aircraft. As a result, the F.E.2Ds were withdrawn from service to allow the supply of engines to be redirected.

A total of 248 F.E.2Ds were built, 189 of these reaching the Western Front. Sergeant Thomas Mottershead was awarded the VC for bringing his burning F.E.2D back for a safe landing despite his burns.

The nacelle was made of wood and canvas, and as might be expected, the wings were wood and fabric. The wingspan was 47ft 9in (14.55m) and the length was 32ft 3in (9.83m). The F.E.2D stood at a height of 12ft 8in (3.86m).

Royal Aircraft Factory R.E.7

Designed by the Royal Aircraft Factory as a reconnaissance and light bomber aircraft, the R.E.7 emerged as a two-seat machine developed from an earlier aircraft, the R.E.5. The R.E.7 first flew in 1915 and was ordered into quantity production, with sub-contractors including Coventry Ordnance Works, Austin Motor Company, Napier and Siddeley-Deasy. A total of 230 would be built for the RFC. It became operational with the RFC in France in early 1916.

It was conventionally constructed of wood and fabric with a wingspan of 57ft (17.37m) and a length of 31ft 10½in (9.69m).

The early examples were powered by a 120hp (89kW) Beardmore motor, but it became apparent that the single Lewis machine gun fitted to the R.E.7 did not give sufficient field of fire for the machine to be used for escort duties. However, the R.E.7 had a useful payload and therefore lent itself more usefully as a light bomber, particularly when more powerful engines were installed. These were either the 150hp (112kW) R.A.F.4a or the 160hp (119kW) Beardmore. With the R.A.F. motor, top speed was 84mph (134km/h), but the service ceiling was only 6,500ft (1,981m).

By the middle of 1916, there were many R.E.7s operational in France, but the low speed and poor ceiling meant that they were increasingly vulnerable to attack. They were soon withdrawn from frontline service but continued in a training role as well as acting as engine test beds and even as tugs for target drones.

The Royal Aircraft Factory R.E.7. (*Flight* via Key Archives)

Royal Aircraft Factory F.E.8

The F.E.8 was another product of the Royal Aircraft Factory. In design, it was very similar to the DH2, a single-seat pusher with a single Lewis machine gun situated in the front of the cockpit, on a special pivot enabling some deflection in firing. It was designed by Henry Folland who would go on to be chief designer at Gloster Aircraft Company and, later, set up Folland Aircraft Ltd where his last design was the forerunner of the Folland Gnat.

The prototype's first flight was on 15 October 1915. Additional fuel capacity was installed to meet the requirements of the RFC and the aircraft was then ordered into production. Construction was subcontracted to Vickers and the Darracq Motor Engineering Company, but delivery was slow and the similar DH2 was delivered some months before.

The F.E.8 wings were constructed with a wooden frame and fabric covering. The nacelle was an all-metal structure with a steel tube framework covered with duralumin. The tail booms, like the F.E.2B, were constructed of wood with wire bracing. The aircraft had good handling characteristics and was light on the controls. However, a rumour that it would be impossible to pull out of a spin was only disproved when a test pilot deliberately engaged in such a manoeuvre and survived. The design, particularly of the tail skid assembly, resulted in maintenance issues.

Like other pusher-design aircraft, the F.E.8 proved vulnerable to the more advanced German fighters, although there is evidence that an F.E.8 was responsible for shooting down Manfred von Richthofen by piercing his fuel tank, leading to a forced landing and a narrow escape.

Power for the F.E.8 came from a 100hp (75kW) Gnome Monosoupape rotary engine, which gave a top speed of 94.5mph (151km/h). During 1916, 103 F.E.8 aircraft were delivered to France.

The F.E.8 was gradually withdrawn from service and squadrons re-equipped with newer tractor aircraft. The last squadron using them did so for ground-attack operations during the Battle of Messines in Flanders. The F.E.8 was the last of the pusher fighters/scouts to see service when the newer designs of tractor aircraft appeared. By August 1917, the F.E.8 had been withdrawn from operational service.

A Royal Aircraft Factory F.E.8 shot down Manfred von Richthofen's aircraft. (Frank R. Mormillo via *Aeroplane* via Key Archives)

Handley Page O/100

The O/100 was produced in 1915 in response to an Admiralty specification. This itself was the result of discussions between the director of the Royal Navy Air Department and Frederick Handley Page (later Sir Frederick Handley Page). The Navy wanted a long-range bomber that would be able to make a significant impact on the war, particularly the ability to bomb the German High Seas Fleet at its base in Kiel. The Navy had a natural inclination towards a large seaplane but was persuaded that a large land-based aircraft would be the solution.

A specification to this effect was issued on 28 December 1914 for four prototypes. The specification called for a twin-engine aircraft to be powered by 150hp (110kW) Sunbeam engines. A specific requirement was for the wings to be capable of being folded in order to fit a 75 x 75ft (23 x 23m) hangar. It was required to carry six bombs, each weighing 100lb (45kg), and have armour protection for the crew and engines. The only defensive armament envisaged at this stage seems to have been a rifle for the observer. In early February 1915, the design was approved and an order for an additional eight aircraft was issued. The powerplant was amended to the 250hp (190kW) Rolls-Royce Eagle engine.

It was the largest aircraft that had been built in Great Britain and, indeed, one of the largest in the world at that time. It was the first of a long line of heavy bombers designed and built by Handley Page at Cricklewood.

The wings were the standard wooden structure, fabric covered, but the fuselage incorporated some plywood covering. This was a large aircraft, with an upper wingspan of 100ft (30.48m) and a lower span of 70ft (21.34m). The length of the aircraft was 62ft 10in (19.15m).

The first prototype had its maiden flight on 17 December 1915. This was a short straight flight. The next day it took off again, but this time it was found that the aircraft could not fly faster than about 55mph (89km/h). It was thought to be due to drag from the large radiators, which were changed from large flat-fronted radiators to tubular radiators on each side of the engine nacelles.

The first three aircraft were the subject of considerable experimentation during 1916 and some issues with the tail assembly caused concern. At 70mph (110km/h) the tail unit began to vibrate and twist violently, and on landing, inspection showed damage to the structure. There were also some control problems with heavy ailerons and elevators and an over-balanced rudder. When reinforcement failed to cure the problems, changes were made with a longer nose, elimination of much of the armour plating and an open, rather than enclosed, cockpit.

After further tests, the aircraft was accepted by the RNAS for additional trials. These revealed continuing problems with tail oscillation and directional stability. Additional bracing of the rear fuselage eventually cured this problem and once rectified, 46 Handley Page O/100s were built with the bulk having more powerful 320hp (239kW) Rolls-Royce Eagle engines. The aircraft had a crew of four or five and was armed with five Lewis machine guns, two in the nose, two in dorsal positions and one in a ventral hatch.

Twenty O/100s were sent to France in late 1916. Initially these were employed in daylight operations over the North Sea, but the loss of one aircraft to an enemy fighter meant a switch to night operations. Some aircraft were based on the east coast of England for anti-U-boat patrols.

An O/100 was flown 2,000 miles (3,218km) from England to the Greek island of Lemnos to support the campaign against Ottoman Empire forces in the Dardanelles. It also assisted in supporting the Arab insurgency being orchestrated by T.E. Lawrence. Through July, August and September 1917, the aircraft was active in bombing raids on Constantinople and other Turkish targets, sinking and damaging shipping. On 30 September, after a bombing raid on railway assets near Constantinople, an engine failure forced the aircraft to ditch in the Gulf of Xeros (Saros). The crew managed to float with the aircraft for two hours, but were eventually obliged to swim ashore where they were captured.

The Handley Page O/100 was Britain's first long-range heavy bomber. (Picryl)

Handley Page O/100 aircraft were used for night-bombing missions during the German Spring Offensive, which began on 21 March 1918. Attacks were made on Cologne railway station, on steel and chemical works and other German strategic targets.

Handley page O/100s served through the remainder of the Great War and were eventually retired in 1921.

A Handley Page O/100 heavy bomber testing engines. (Alamy)

Short Bomber

Short Bros success with the Type S.184 seaplane encouraged the design of a land-based version as a two-seat, long-range reconnaissance, bombing and torpedo-carrying aircraft. In the initial design, the observer/gunner occupied the front cockpit to operate the Lewis machine gun, which was mounted on the upper wing centre section. Unfortunately, this meant standing up to operate it, which was not the ideal arrangement. Before production began, the ring mount had been invented and the cockpit positions were reversed, the pilot occupying the first seat and the observer more comfortably positioned behind.

It was a conventionally constructed wood and fabric aircraft with a wingspan of 84ft (25.6m) and a length of 45ft (13.72m). It had a height of 15ft (4.58m).

Power was provided by the Rolls-Royce Eagle 250hp (186kW) engine, although some aircraft were fitted with Sunbeam engines. In addition to the Lewis gun, the Short Bomber had provision to carry the 14in (0.36m) Whitehead torpedo, or bombs up to 920lb (417kg) in weight. In tests, this bombload proved impossible for the aircraft, so the wingspan was increased by 12ft (3.65m), to give additional lift. This made the machine unstable, so the fuselage was extended by almost 4½ft (1.37m), which solved the problem.

The first flight was in 1915 and large numbers were ordered for the RNAS and RFC from Short's and sub-contractors Mann Egerton & Company, Sunbeam Motor Car Company and Parnall. A total of 83 were built. The top speed was 77mph (123km/h) and the service ceiling was 10,000ft (3,048m).

It entered service in late 1916 and with an endurance of nearly six hours it was ideal for long-range operations, the first being an attack on Ostend in November 1916.

Although bombing operations continued through the 1916–17 winter, the aircraft was underpowered and following a series of raids on Zeebrugge in April 1917 the Short Bomber was withdrawn from service.

The Short Bomber. (Picryl)

Sopwith 1½ Strutter

The Sopwith 1½ Strutter earned its strange name due to the strut arrangement of its upper wing in relation to the fuselage. The upper wing was connected to the fuselage with a short and long strut on each side, looking like a figure 'W' when viewed from the front – hence one and a half.

The Strutter was a two-seat fighter and reconnaissance aircraft, also used for bombing and was the first RFC aircraft to be fitted with interrupter gear to enable its forward-firing Vickers machine gun to fire through the propeller arc. Interrupter gear technology was, inevitably, in its infancy. In December 1915, production of synchronisation gears from Vickers-Challenger for the RFC commenced, followed shortly after by synchronisation equipment from Scarff-Dibovski for the RNAS. Early aircraft were fitted with either, or none at all, which limited armament to the observer's Lewis machine gun. Later Strutters had either the Ross or Sopwith-Kauper synchronisation gears. None were reliable at this time and propellers were sometimes damaged or even shot away by failings in the mechanism.

The rear observer's cockpit was equipped with a Lewis machine gun on a Scarff ring, again a first for a British aircraft. Even more innovative was the provision of trailing edge flaps, although they were called air brakes. The Strutter's construction was very conventional with a wooden framework and fabric covering. Wingspan was 33ft 6in (10.2m) and the length was 25ft 3in (7.7m).

Power came from either a 110 or 130hp (82 or 97kW) Clerget rotary motor, giving the Strutter a top speed of 100mph (160km/h) and an endurance of three hours 45 minutes. The aircraft had notably good handling characteristics, later inherited by the Sopwith Pup.

The prototype first flew in December 1915. The first orders for the Strutter were on behalf of the RNAS, so it was to this service that the first production aircraft were delivered in February 1916. They reached the Western Front in late spring 1916.

Although the War Office had placed orders in March 1916 for deliveries of the Strutter to the RFC, Sopwith's production capacity was fully committed to the RNAS and the RFC production was sub-contracted to Ruston Proctor and Co of Lincoln and to Vickers. Unfortunately, these companies could not achieve full production until August.

The very successful Sopwith 'Strutter'. (Picryl)

Planning for the Battle of the Somme was based on the action taking place from the end of June 1916. This left a serious gap in the RFC's arsenal of modern aircraft. A transfer of Sopwith Strutters from the RNAS to the RFC was agreed, allowing a squadron of Strutters to appear on the battlefield by early July.

Throughout the Battle of the Somme, Strutters were engaged in fighting, strategic reconnaissance, photographic and day-bombing activities. By late autumn 1916, the Strutters were being outmatched by the new German Albatros and Halberstadt fighters. Even so, they continued to be used on photographic and strategic reconnaissance work. The Sopwith Strutter suffered more than any other British aircraft during what became known as 'Bloody April', the Battle of Arras, in April 1917. It was still used operationally during the battles of Arras and Messines (Flanders) until finally relieved in July 1917.

The RNAS used its Strutters as bombers in France, the Aegean and Macedonia. Up to 130lb (60kg) of bombs could be carried. The French Aeronautique Militaire was the largest user of the Sopwith Strutter, with 4,500 being built in France. They were used primarily for attacks on military and industrial targets as well as the German front line. The last Strutters were withdrawn from operational service in early 1918 but continued in training units after the war.

The Strutter had a remarkable production history with 1,439 being built in Britain. Some British-built Strutters were supplied to the Belgian air force. About 100 were built in Russia, one of which was later supplied to the Afghanistan Air Force where it was still in existence in December 1924. The American Expeditionary Force purchased 384 and they were also used by the US Navy.

Other foreign users included the Australian Flying Corps, Belgian Aviation Militaire Belge, Brazilian Escola de Aviacao Militar, Czechoslovak Legion, Estonian Air Force, Hellenic Navy, Imperial Japanese Army Air Service, Latvian Air Force, Lithuanian Air Force, Mexican Arma de Aviacion Militar, Polish Air Force, Romanian Air Corps, Imperial Russian Air Force, White Russian forces and the Soviet Air Force. Five Strutters landed in the neutral Netherlands, where they were interned and subsequently purchased by the Royal Netherlands Air Force.

Sopwith Pup

The Pup earned a well-deserved reputation for having the best handling characteristics of any biplane of its time. It was in many ways the perfect flying machine. Its ancestry began in 1915 when Sopwith designed and built a small, low-powered biplane for the use of Harry Hawker, Sopwith's test pilot. This machine acquired the nickname of 'Hawker's Runabout'. It had a 50hp (37kW) Gnome rotary engine. The next development was a larger version as a fighter, with ailerons rather than wing-warping for control. This machine was armed with a fixed Vickers machine gun with synchronisation.

This aircraft had its first flight in February 1916 and was evaluated by the RNAS. This evaluation report was also seen by the RFC and, as a result, both the RFC and RNAS placed orders for this new aircraft by the end of June. Although initially called the Sopwith Scout, its similarity with the shape of the Sopwith Strutter soon earned the name 'Pup'.

Power was provided either by an 80hp (60kW) Le Rhone rotary engine or 100hp (75kW) Gnome Monosoupape rotary motor. The Le Rhone engine gave a top speed of just over 104mph (166km/h) at an altitude of 10,000ft (3,048m). It had an endurance of three hours. The Pup had a low wing loading, helping it to land in extremely small fields, an asset when operating from rough grass airstrips or when having to force land in tight spaces.

The Pup had spruce main spars for the wings with fabric covering. The centre section was covered with celluloid to improve the pilot's upward vision. The fuselage was wooden with a fabric covering, the

The Sopwith Pup was 'the perfect flying machine'. (Roger Staker)

motor bearers were ash attached to a steel torque plate and fireproof bulkhead. The wingspan was 26ft 6in (8.08m), and the length was 19ft 4in (5.89m). Fuel capacity was 18 gallons (81 litres/22 US gallons).

The RNAS Pup first appeared on the Western Front in early September 1916 and scored its first success on 24 September by shooting down a German LVG two-seater aircraft. The RFC's Sopwith Pups arrived in France in December of that year, and proved their worth in the battles of Ypres, Messines and Cambrai. They were one of the few British aircraft of that time with performance equal to the German Albatros Scout. They could also hold their height better than the enemy aircraft.

By mid-1917, the Sopwith Pup had become outclassed by the newer German fighters and it was also under-armed. The Pup was equipped with a single Vickers machine gun firing through the propeller arc via synchronisation gear. Some RNAS machines had a Lewis gun instead, and some were also equipped with external racks to hold four bombs, each 25lb (11.4kg). The last frontline squadron operating the Sopwith Pup had its aircraft replaced by Sopwith Camels in December 1917 and the RNAS had also phased out its Pups by late 1917.

In mid-1917, London was suffering from bombing raids by German Gotha bombers. Sopwith Pups were utilised for home defence duties to counter the threat.

The RNAS experimented with deck-flying as an alternative to the time-consuming and risky process of using hoists to transfer seaplanes from ship to sea and back again. The first objective was to launch an aircraft from the deck of a ship. The Pup was an ideal aircraft for such a challenge and in June 1917 Flight Commander F.J. Rutland flew a Pup off a 20ft (6.1m) platform fixed to the top of a gun turret on the light cruiser HMS *Yarmouth*. It was the first such flight.

In August 1917, a Sopwith Pup became the first aircraft to land on a moving ship, when Squadron Commander Edwin Dunning landed on HMS *Furious*. Sadly, he was killed on his third landing when the aircraft toppled over the side of the ship. Nevertheless, the potential had been proved and Pups, equipped with arrester gear systems, were used as ship-borne fighters by the RNAS from early 1917.

Aviation history resources vary in their estimate of the total number of Sopwith Pups built, ranging from 1,301 to 1,847. The truth is probably somewhere in between.

The Pup was deployed by the Australian Flying Corps, Australian Air Force, Belgian Air Force, Hellenic Navy, Imperial Japanese Navy and Imperial Japanese Army, Royal Netherlands Air Force, Romanian Air Corps, Imperial Russian Air Force and Soviet Air Force.

Martinsyde Elephant (G.100 and G.102)

The Elephant was designed and built by Martin & Handasyde, which was based in Brooklands and Woking in Surrey. The name was never formally approved by the company or the government, but it stuck. Strangely, the aircraft is immortalised with an elephant in the crest of No. 27 Squadron, which flew its Martinsydes (not then called Elephants) to France at the beginning of March 1916.

Martin & Handasyde recruited Sydney Camm as a carpenter's apprentice in 1913. He would later become famous as the designer of the Hawker Hurricane. The prototype, powered by a 120hp (89kW) Austro-Daimler engine, began testing in the autumn of 1915.

The Elephant was entirely standard in its construction, so Sydney Camm's carpentry skills would have been appropriate. The Elephant had a wingspan of 38ft 1in (11.61m), and a length of 27ft (8.23m). The relatively large size of the aircraft met with disapproval because it was believed to limit manoeuvrability.

The Martinsyde Elephant was designed as a single-seat fighter and also a day bomber. It was armed with a Lewis machine gun on a mounting above the wing centre section and fired above the arc of the propeller. A second Lewis machine gun was mounted on the starboard side of the cockpit, which enabled the pilot to fire backwards against pursuing aircraft. It could carry a single 112lb (246kg) bomb under the fuselage.

Power was provided by a 120hp (89kW) six-cylinder Beardmore motor, and for the G.102 the motor was a 160hp (119kW) Beardmore. The G.100 had a top speed of 95mph (152km/h), while the higher-powered G.102 could manage 102mph (163km/h). With an endurance of 4 hours 30 minutes, the Elephant was very suitable for long-range operations.

The Martinsyde Elephant fighter. (Picryl)

The Elephant was credited with fine handling characteristics and was a pleasant aircraft to fly. A disadvantage was that it tended to 'float' just before touch-down when landing, which is probably a tribute to its clean and streamlined design.

Although intended as a fighter/scout, the Elephant did not perform well in this role, and was used for reconnaissance and photographic functions, as well as bombing. During the Battle of the Somme (July to November 1916), Elephants were used for bombing raids behind the German front lines. They proved to be so successful at this that all future 160hp Beardmore aircraft were converted to fighter-bombers. During the 1916–17 winter, offensive operations were resumed but bombing remained the key function as the German army retreated to the Hindenburg Line, as in the Battle of Arras.

No. 27 squadron developed tactics for low-level flying, making use of rain, low clouds and haze to escape detection. This technique was used to good effect during the Third Battle of Ypres when Elephants often bombed enemy troops and aerodromes from as low as 100ft (30.5m).

A total of 271 Elephants were built. Of these, 137 were deployed on the Western Front and a further 68 were used in Egypt and the Middle East. The remainder were issued to training units, although one was tested for Home Defence operations. In addition to the RFC, the Australian Flying Corps used the Martinsyde Elephants in Egypt and Palestine. In July 1917, the Elephants were replaced with new models of aircraft.

A Martinsyde Elephant shows its clean lines. (Johan Visschedijk, 1000aircraftphotos.com)

Royal Aircraft Factory R.E.8

The R.E.8 was a product of the Royal Aircraft Factory, but it was also manufactured by the Austin Motor Company, the Standard Motor Company, Daimler, Siddeley-Deasy and the Coventry Ordnance Works. It was designed as a two-seat reconnaissance aircraft to replace the ageing and increasingly unpopular B.E.2c and B.E.2e aircraft. Shortages of materials meant that the R.E.8s did not reach the Western Front until late in 1916, too late to have any real impact on the Battle of the Somme, which began on 1 July 1916.

There were numerous teething problems, resulting in many pilots being killed before the Air Board ordered certain defects to be remedied. One problem that could lead to disaster was a tendency to 'buck' when landing due to the high angle with which the aircraft presented to the ground, a deliberate design feature intended to shorten the landing run. The early versions were considered dangerous to fly and allegedly dangerous to spin and liable to break up in a dive. The R.E.8 even became the subject of a lively debate in Parliament. The R.E.8's reputation was never entirely eliminated.

Design work commenced in the latter part of 1915, and like earlier Royal Aircraft Factory designs, the philosophy behind the design was inbuilt stability in order to fulfil an observation role. Unfortunately, this was a pre-war concept that did not meet the requirements of the actual events taking place in the air over the Western Front. However, real efforts had been made to address the criticisms of the B.E.2 in terms of performance and payload, so the observer did not need to be left behind when the aircraft was required to carry bombs or even a full load of fuel.

By April 1916, the mock-up shape and equipment of the R.E.8 had been decided, including the choice of engine, which was to be the Royal Aircraft Factory 4a air-cooled engine. Two prototypes were in production and on 17 June the first prototype took to the air, followed on 16 July by the second prototype. This second aircraft was sent to France for service trials, which were generally successful. On its return to Britain, some modifications were made based on that experience.

The R.E.8 incorporated some innovation, including the ability for the pilot to adjust the incidence of the tailplane in flight, and a basic form of trim control designed to help the pilot by relieving him of constant pressure on the controls. Flight controls for the elevators, rudder and throttle were fitted

A Royal Aircraft Factory R.E.8, an aircraft debated in Parliament. (Picryl)

in the observer's cockpit, providing the possibility of making a forced landing if the pilot were to be incapacitated.

The R.E.8 was powered by a 150hp (112kW) Royal Aircraft Factory 4a 12-cylinder engine providing a top speed of 102mph (163km/h) and an endurance of more than four hours. The wings had spruce spars and were fabric covered, but the upper and lower centre sections were celluloid covered to improve visibility. The R.E.8 had an upper wingspan of 42ft 7in (12.97m), a lower wingspan of 32ft 7½in (9.96m) and a length of 27ft 10in (8.5m).

The aircraft was built in substantial numbers, with more than 4,000 being constructed. Of these, more than 2,000 were deployed to the Western Front. Others saw service in Russia, Palestine and Mesopotamia. The R.E.8 was equipped with a fixed Vickers machine gun, synchronised to fire through the propeller arc, and either a single or double Lewis machine gun on a Scarff ring for the observer in the rear cockpit.

Despite the challenges the aircraft and crews faced, the R.E.8s performed a vast number of artillery observations against dreadful anti-aircraft fire. They probably clocked up more hours in the air than any other type. They were also the pioneers of radio communications.

Given the obvious vulnerability of an aircraft tasked with flying slow and flat over enemy lines, casualties were high. A method of defence evolved, which meant flying the aircraft as slowly as possible so that the enemy fighters 'overshot' their prey and became sitting ducks for the rear gunner.

Despite the R.E.8 being scheduled for replacement by Bristol Fighters, none had been delivered to the squadrons by the time of the Armistice in November 1918. Other users of the R.E.8 included the Australian Flying Corps, Belgian Aviation Militaire Belge, Estonian Air Force and Soviet Union.

Royal Aircraft Factory B.E.12

The B.E.12 was a short-lived expedient by the Royal Aircraft Factory to produce a single-seat fighter/scout. With the benefit of hindsight and the absence of war pressures, it is easy to be critical of what now looks like a clumsy approach to a real challenge. The B.E.12 appeared at a difficult time for the RFC and RNAS. War in the air had changed from reconnaissance and observation to bombing and firing at each other's aircraft.

On 1 August 1915, a step-change took place when Max Immelmann, flying a Fokker Eindekker equipped with synchronisation gear, shot down a British aircraft that was bombing Douai aerodrome, France. It was not until December 1915 that the first British aircraft with synchronisation of the forward-firing machine gun had its first flight. It was therefore not until the late spring of 1916 that the Fokker scourge came to an end, when sufficient numbers of suitably equipped Allied aircraft came into service.

The B.E.12 was produced by taking a B.E.2c airframe, substituting the 90hp (67kW) Royal Aircraft Factory 1 motor for a 150hp (112kW) Royal Aircraft Factory 4a motor and fairing over the observer's cockpit, within which was now fitted a large fuel tank. The aircraft was made of wood with a fabric covering, the wingspan was 37ft (11.28m) and the length was 27ft 3in (8.3m).

Armament was either one or two Lewis machine guns mounted outside the pilot's cockpit and splayed outwards away from the aircraft in order to clear the propeller arc. This meant that the pilot had to fly the aircraft in a crab-like manner when attacking an enemy aircraft. It has been strongly suggested that the Royal Aircraft Factory B.E.12 did not compare favourably with aircraft being designed and built by private sector companies.

B.E.12s were introduced to the Western Front shortly before the Battle of the Somme in 1916. The serious limitations imposed by the gun arrangements were soon obvious and the positive response was

The Royal Aircraft Factory B.E.12, which was not a solution to a problem. (Chaz Bowyer via *Flight* via Key Archives)

the fitting of a Vickers machine gun with interrupter gear. Even so, it was clear that the B.E.12 was simply outclassed as a fighter and was relegated to day- and night-bombing raids with suitable escorts.

Some B.E.2e two-seater aircraft were modified and became known as the B.E.12a. These had the wings of the B.E.2e and were more manoeuvrable, but otherwise displayed little improvement. The B.E.12b was a version based on the B.E.2c airframe, but with a 200hp (149kW) Hispano-Suiza engine. This had wing-mounted Lewis machine guns in place of the Vickers machine gun and was intended as a night fighter. Since engines were more urgently required for the newer S.E.5. only a few were delivered to squadrons for home defence. Some B.E.12b aircraft were never fitted with engines.

Altogether, about 468 B.E.12, B.E.12a and B.E.12b aircraft were built with 130 deployed on the Western Front. A further 67 saw service in the Middle East, 101 on Home Defence duties and 170 were allocated to training establishments. By December 1916, the majority of remaining B.E.12s on the Western Front had been withdrawn.

The B.E.12 had a relatively short life as a front-line fighter. (Picryl, public domain)

Airco DH6

The Aircraft Manufacturing Company's DH6 was designed from the outset as a trainer, although it also featured later as an anti-submarine patrol aircraft. It acquired the nickname 'Clutching Hand'. A very unusual feature was that the upper and lower wings were square-cut and interchangeable, leading to the myth that they were 'made by the mile and cut-off by the yard (metre)'. Geoffrey de Havilland wanted to make the aircraft inexpensive to build and maintain, an important factor for a dedicated trainer where minor incidents were likely to occur on a frequent basis. The instructor and pupil were seated in tandem on wicker/basketwork seats in a single cockpit.

Another unusual feature was the option for the instructor to decouple the pupil's controls if needed to prevent two 'pilots' wrestling with opposing views of what to do. The DH6 was extremely safe, stable and forgiving. It could fly at just 30mph (48km/h) and poor use of the rudder in turns might provoke a crab-like flight path but not cause a disaster. It was an efficient training aircraft with no vices, but considered by some to be too lenient on inexperienced pilots. The shape of the wings limited manoeuvrability.

Its structure was an entirely standard wooden framework with fabric covering. The wingspan was 35ft 11in (10.98m), and the length was 27ft 3½in (8.35m).

The DH6 first flew in 1916, with nearly 1,500 DH6 trainers in service by 1918. Equipped with a single 90hp (67kW) Royal Aircraft Factory 1a engine, it was not quick, having a top speed of just 66mph (106km/h). When supplies of the R.A.F. engines were in short supply other engines were fitted including an 80hp (60kW) Renault, and an American Curtiss OX-5 liquid-cooled engine.

The DH6 was superseded by the Avro 504K, and the now redundant DH6s were reissued to the RNAS for anti-submarine patrol work and based on the east coast of Britain. More than 300 were assigned to this role. For anti-submarine work, the DH6 was fitted with racks for light bombs to be carried under the wings. Although the aircraft with the R.A.F. engines proved reliable, there were problems with the Curtiss OX-5 motors. The reliability was poor and forced descents into the sea were not unusual. Fortunately, the DH6 could stay afloat for ten hours so many lives were saved. On the negative side, the aircraft could not carry bombs at the same time as an observer so even if a submarine was identified, the aircraft was powerless to attack.

At least 2,282 DH6 aircraft were built, 342 being issued to training units in 1917 and another 1,189 in 1918. In addition to Airco, DH6 aircraft were manufactured by Graham-White, Kingsbury Aviation, Harland & Wolff, Ransomes, Sims & Jefferies, and Gloster Aircraft Company.

Home Defence accounted for 71, and 27 were sent to the Middle East.

The 'Clutching Hand', an Airco DH6. (Picryl)

Bristol Fighter Type F.2B

In the second half of 1915, the RFC was in need of a new reconnaissance and artillery-spotting aircraft to replace the ageing B.E.2c. A key attribute required was the ability to defend itself in the air. Several aircraft were developed to meet the requirements, notably the R.E.8 from the Royal Aircraft Factory and the Armstrong Whitworth proposal that became the F.K.8.

In March 1916, the Bristol Aeroplane Company began work on a B.E.2 replacement. The design was in two parts, the R.2A, to be powered by an 120hp (88kW) Beardmore engine, and the R.2B with a 150hp (110kW) Hispano-Suiza engine. The designs showed the fuselage mounted between the wings with a gap between the bottom of the fuselage and the lower wing together with part of the fin under the fuselage. These features were intended to improve the pilot's visibility as well as the observer's field of fire. Pilot and observer were placed close together for ease of communication.

Before either of these were built, a new engine, the 190hp (142kW) Rolls-Royce Falcon in-line engine, became available. This changed the potential usage for the Bristol. Instead of replacing the relatively mundane role of the B.E.2, the potential now was to replace the F.E.2D and the Sopwith 1½ Strutter. Construction of a pair of prototypes began in July 1916 and an initial contract for 50 production aircraft was issued in August.

The first prototype, powered by the Falcon engine, had its first flight on 9 September 1916. In order to save time, the wings were from the B.E.2d, Bristol being a sub-contractor for the type. In late October, the second prototype was complete. Flight testing showed that the radiator obscured the pilot's view and so the nose was redesigned. Official trials were undertaken at the Central Flying School between 16 and 18 October. A variety of propeller configurations were tested.

The first 52 aircraft were designated Bristol F.2As. The main production aircraft was the F.2B, the first 150 of which were powered by either the Rolls-Royce Falcon I or the Falcon II engines. Subsequent aircraft were powered by the 275hp (205kW) Rolls-Royce Falcon III. This engine added 10mph (16km/h) to the top speed and improved the rate of climb.

The aircraft was built by the British and Colonial Aeroplane Company in Bristol and also by a sub-contractor, the National Aircraft Factory at Aintree, near Liverpool. Eventually, other sub-contractors were involved including Standard Motors, Armstrong Whitworth and the Cunard Steamship Company.

The Bristol Fighter was powered by one of three engines as the Rolls-Royce engines were in short supply, a 200hp (149kW) Sunbeam Arab, a 200hp (149kW) Hispano-Suiza or the 275hp (205kW) Rolls-Royce Falcon III motor (Bristol Fighter F. 2C). The Falcon gave the Bristol Fighter a top speed of 125mph (200km/h), while the alternative engines meant a top speed of 105mph (168km/h). Endurance was three hours.

Wings were made of spruce with a fabric covering. The fuselage forward of the pilot's cockpit was metal covered, with more traditional fabric covering elsewhere. The wingspan was 39ft 4in (11.99m). The length with the Falcon engine was 26ft 2in (7.97m) and with the Hispano engine it was 24ft 9in (7.54m).

Armament was a Vickers machine gun synchronised to fire through the propeller arc and either a single or twin Lewis machine gun on a Scarff ring for the observer. The Bristol Fighter could carry light fragmentation bombs on racks under the inner bays of the wings. For ground attack or so-called 'contact patrols' three 20lb (9kg) bombs could be deployed.

The first Bristol Fighters to reach the RFC were delivered just before Christmas 1916. They were transferred to France in March 1917. At this point, the tide of war was starting to turn in favour of the Allies, although 'Bloody April' was imminent. In 1917, German aircraft manufacturers produced 13,977 machines while Britain produced 13,766, and France manufactured 14,915. German aero-engine production slumped to 12,029 whereas Britain and France combined to produce nearly 25,000. However, it was difficult to dismiss the quality of the German products.

The Bristol Type F.2B Fighter, possibly the best all-round aircraft of the Great War. (Roger Staker)

Into this stage of the war came the Bristol Fighter, recognised as a superb fighting machine, and possibly the finest all-round aircraft of the Great War. Although a two-seater, the Bristol Fighter could be flown and operated like a single-seat fighter aircraft.

During the Battle of Arras in April 1917, a flight of six Bristol Fighters was savaged by the Red Baron's squadron, with four of the Bristols shot down. It seems that the British crews were treating the F.2 like previous generations of two-seater reconnaissance aircraft, trying to hold a formation while the observers/gunners attempted to hold off the attacking Albatros fighter. Once recognised for its capabilities, the tables were turned as the crews realised the ability of the Bristol Fighter to be handled like a single-seat fighter, and began to be used in that way.

After the first disappointing skirmish, the aircraft was recognised as a first class fighting/reconnaissance machine and substantial orders were placed. In the autumn of 1917 alone, these orders numbered 1,600. When the US entered the war, it had no combat aircraft of significance. The Bristol Fighter was quickly seen as the answer and production of the aircraft began in earnest in the US. An order for 1,000 was placed with American companies, which doubled to 2,000 in late 1917.

Unfortunately, political and other vested interests intervened. American influencers demanded the choice of engine should be the American 400hp (298kW) Liberty L-12, which was far too heavy for the Bristol Fighter. After contracts were placed, then cancelled, and different manufacturers appointed, then changed, the result was that only about 25 aircraft were completed by the Armistice and none saw service in France.

At the end of the war, the RAF still had 1,583 Bristol Fighters in service in France, the Middle East, Italy and in Home Defence roles. A total of 5,329 Bristol Fighters were eventually built. After the Great War, Bristol Fighters continued in service with the RAF and with the air forces of Australia, New Zealand, Belgium, Canada, Ireland, Greece, Spain, Norway, Peru, Mexico and Sweden. The RAF withdrew its remaining Bristol Fighters in 1932, but it remained in service until 1935 in New Zealand.

Blackburn T.B.15

On the night of 19 January 1915, the first Zeppelin raid on Britain took place when the towns of Great Yarmouth and King's Lynn on the Norfolk coast were bombed. Although deaths were low at four people, the shock and public anger was understandable as no-one could have imagined that the country could be attacked from the air. During May 1915, London was attacked and there were many more civilian deaths.

To counter the Zeppelin threat, the British Admiralty issued a specification for a two-seat long-range/endurance interceptor/fighter that would drop Ranken darts onto the Zeppelins from above. These darts were bombs with a spring-loaded vaned tail that contained 1lb (450g) of explosives. They were 13in long (330mm) and 5⁹⁄₁₀in (150mm) wide. The intention was to penetrate the Zeppelin's envelope and ignite the supporting gas.

The T.B.15 was Blackburn's first twin-engine aircraft, but was remarkable in actually having two fuselages, each with its own engine. The fuselages were 10ft (3.35m) apart, one containing the pilot and the other accommodating the observer. As a result, there was no means of communication between them, except perhaps for hand signals but at night these would have been of limited value.

The aircraft was an all-wooden construction except for steel pylons above the upper wing, which provided support for bracing wires. The original intention was to have 150hp (112kW) Smith engines, which were of an American design and held out the promise of low fuel consumption and light weight. The engine did not prove a success and the first T.B.15 to fly had 100hp (75kW) Gnome Monosoupape 9 Type B-2 engines. This had its first flight in August 1915.

During 1916, T.B.15s, including one example powered by Clerget engines, were evaluated by the RNAS at the Marine Experimental Aircraft Depot. Wing flexibility caused some problems with the aileron cables becoming slack, resulting in poor lateral control, which was soon rectified. Otherwise, the aircraft flew successfully but with poor performance due to the low power of the engines.

The T.B.15 was unarmed except for the Ranken incendiary darts. Again, the poor engine power limited its potential, being able to carry only 70lb (32kg) of bombs and sufficient fuel for four hours of flight.

A total of nine aircraft were built, seven of them being delivered to RNAS KIllinghome, Lincolnshire, and the remaining two delivered to store. Little service seems to have taken place and all the aircraft had been broken up by August 1917.

The Blackburn T.B.15 had a top speed of 86mph (138km/h). It took 12 minutes to climb to 5,000ft (1,534m) so its ability to intercept and climb above incoming Zeppelins is possibly unrealistic. Its wingspan was 60ft 6in (18.44m) and its length was 36ft 6in (11.13m).

The highly unusual Blackburn T.B.15 saw little service. (Johan Visschenijk, 1000aircraftphotos.com)

Felixstowe Porte Baby

This large flying boat takes its name from John Cyril Porte, who had served with the Royal Navy until he was invalided out in 1911. After working in America with Glenn Curtiss on the design of flying boats, he returned to England at the outbreak of the Great War and took command of the RNAS base at Felixstowe.

Porte embarked on a completely new aircraft of his own design, inevitably nicknamed 'Porte Baby'. It was to be a large aircraft.

The prototype was powered by three 250hp (186kW) Rolls-Royce engines, the central motor in pusher mode and the outer two operating in tractor mode. The enclosed cockpit carried two pilots and the remaining three crew members were in open cockpits. Its first flight was on 20 November 1915. There were problems in the water, which were resolved by extending the bow by 3ft (0.9m), and it was underpowered, achieving only 78mph (125km/h).

Ten production aircraft were ordered, fitted with Rolls-Royce Eagle engines of either 345hp (257kW) or 360hp (268kW). Although there was an improvement in performance, it was not deemed to be sufficient to commit to a large production order. The production aircraft, which had been ordered were delivered from May 1916 to March 1917. Porte's 'Babies' were deployed on anti-submarine patrols from British bases.

It proved itself to be a rugged and robust aircraft. An attack on a Porte Baby by two German seaplanes and a landplane in October 1917 damaged two of the three engines, forcing the aircraft to land whereupon it was subjected to further attacks. Despite this, the crew were able to undertake sufficient repair work on the engines to enable the Baby to taxi slowly across the North Sea to the safety of the coast in Suffolk.

It was a significantly larger aircraft than the Felixstowe F.2A, with a wingspan of 124ft (37.8m) and a length of 63ft (19.21m). Between November 1915 and the Armistice, it was Britain's largest flying boat.

The prototype was used for a variety of experiments including carrying two torpedoes at the same time. The most extraordinary feature of all was carrying a Bristol Scout fighter aircraft in 'piggy-back' form on its upper wing. On 17 May 1916, this combination took off and at 1,000ft (305m) the Scout detached and flew back safely.

With three 345hp (257kW) Rolls-Royce Eagle VII engines, the maximum speed was 87.5mph (141km/h) and it had a service ceiling of 8,000ft (2,440m). Defensive armament was three Lewis machine guns, one in the nose and two amidships.

A Felixstowe Porte Baby with a Scout fighter carried on the upper wing. (Picryl)

Vickers F.B.14

The Vickers F.B.14 was designed as a two-seat fighter and reconnaissance aircraft. The intended powerplant was a 230hp (170kW) Beardmore-Halford-Pullinger in-line engine, which was a new development. The airframe was a steel tube construction with the pilot sitting underneath the upper wing. Visibility for the pilot was provided by transparent panels in the upper wing centre section and the lower wing roots, enabling some upward and downwards vision. It was armed with a fixed forward-firing Vickers machine gun and a single Lewis machine gun on a Scarff ring in the rear cockpit.

The aircraft was completed in mid-1916, but the intended engine was still not available. Instead, it was fitted with a 160hp (120kW) Beardmore engine. Not surprisingly it was under-powered and there were also reliability problems. Even so, the Vickers F.B.14 went into production and more than 50 were delivered to the RFC without engines.

A variety of engines were tried, including 150hp (112kW) Lorraine-Dietrich, 250hp (186kW) Rolls-Royce Eagle IV, and 150hp (112kW) R.A.F. 4A engines.

About 100 F.B.14 aircraft were built, of various designations depending on the engine installed, but only about half of these were fitted with engines, the remainder going to store. There was very limited operational use, a few being assigned to Home Defence squadrons and some were sent to Mesopotamia. On 17 July 1917, an experimental F.B.14 fitted with a Rolls-Royce engine was involved in the interception of a Gotha bomber returning from a raid on London. Although it was claimed that the Gotha was shot down near Zeebrugge, this could not be confirmed.

With the 160hp (120kW) Beardmore engine, the aircraft had a top speed of 99mph (160km/h) and a service ceiling of 10,000ft (3,000m). The wingspan was 39ft 6in (12.04m) and the length was 28ft 5in (8.66m).

Many Vickers F.B.14 fighters were never fitted with engines. (Alamy)

Vickers F.B.19 Bullet

Towards the end of 1914, the chief test pilot with Vickers, Harold Barnwell, designed a single-seat scout aircraft and had it built without the knowledge of his employers. He 'borrowed' a Gnome Monosoupape rotary engine from Vickers' stores and in early 1915 he attempted his first flight in the machine. It crashed and was wrecked. The suggestion is that Barnwell had misjudged or miscalculated the centre of gravity, making the machine unflyable.

Barnwell's secret was now out, and Vickers' junior designer was instructed to redesign what had become known as Barnwell's Bullet. What emerged was a single-seat fighter designated the Vickers E.S.1, with the pilot's cockpit located underneath the trailing edge of the upper wing, making visibility both upwards and downwards poor. It had its first flight in August 1915.

The E.S.1 was fast, with Vickers claiming 118mph (190km/h). Operational trials took place in France with the aircraft unarmed, following which a modified engine cowling was fitted to prevent what was feared to be potential build-up of fuel in the cowling with a consequent fire risk. It was then armed with a single fixed forward-firing Vickers synchronised machine gun. Two more aircraft were built, this time powered by 110hp (82kW) Clerget engines. The fuselage was modified and a large cut-out in the upper wing improved the pilot's visibility. No production orders were placed as the aircraft was deemed tiring to fly and difficult to land, probably because of the poor downward visibility.

However, from these experiences, Vickers developed a more significant fighter called the Vickers Bullet. Like its predecessor, it was a compact aircraft with a wingspan of only 24ft (7.32m) and a length of 18ft 2in (5.54m). Its 100hp (75kW) Gnome Monosoupape rotary engine gave it a top speed of 102mph (164km/h). The position of the cockpit still limited vision downwards, but a transparent section in the upper wing helped with upward vision. It had its first flight in August 1916.

Six early production examples were sent to France later that year for evaluation under operational conditions. They were not well received and were returned to Britain. Fitted with either the 110hp (82kW) Le Rhone or Clerget engines, about 12 Bullets were sent to the Middle East, five to Palestine and seven to Macedonia. Some served as trainers and for home defence purposes. Before the end of 1917 they had all been retired.

A single example had been sent to Russia in 1916 for evaluation. It seems that between 20 and 30 Bullets were delivered to Russia where they were re-engined with 130hp (97kW) Clerget engines, which raised the top speed to 125mph (200km/h). The Vickers Bullet remained in service in Russia until 1924.

The Vickers Bullet fighter was more popular in Russia than in Britain. (via Key Archives)

Handley Page O/400

The testing and operations of the O/100 resulted directly in the O/400, which had similar dimensions to the O/100 but benefitted from having a newer version of the Rolls-Royce Eagle powerplants, the beginning of a family of aero engines from this manufacturer bearing the names of birds of prey. Two of these engines, each rated at 275hp (205kW), gave the O/400 a top speed of 97mph (155km/h). Like the O/100, the propellers rotated in opposite directions to counteract torque. Construction was wood and fabric with some plywood covering on the fuselage and some armour plating for crew protection.

The bombing squadrons of the RNAS were the first to be equipped with the O/400, based in Dunkirk. The aircraft had folding wings, enabling it to be stored in canvas hangars used on all the grass airfields in France. The aircraft was used in daylight operations over the sea in early 1917, but it came into its own when deployed as a night bomber on raids to Ostend and Zeebrugge, and also against the home bases of German Gotha bombers that were attacking Britain.

In September 1917, the RFC ordered the O/400 for use as a night bomber, apparently following Sir Douglas Haig's demand that a significant proportion of bombing raids on enemy targets should be conducted at night.

The Handley Page O/400 heavy bomber was an updated development of the O/100. (Picryl)

The O/400 was well armed. There was either a single or double Lewis machine gun mounted on a Scarff ring for the bomb aimer/gunner seated in the nose cockpit. The rear cockpit was equipped with either a single Lewis gun mounted on a flexible rocker or two separate Lewis guns on separate brackets on each side of the cockpit. In addition, a Lewis machine gun was fitted to operate through a trapdoor in the floor of the aircraft just behind the wings. Some experimental versions of the aircraft were fitted with six-pounder and two-pounder Davis guns.

Bombs were carried internally, the usual load being either 16 bombs weighing 112lb (51kg) each or eight bombs weighing 250lb (114kg) each. The bombs were held vertically by their noses. The bomb aimer had external bomb sights fitted on the aircraft nose, and additional sights were provided under the pilot's seat.

With an upper wingspan of 100ft (30.5m), the O/400 was a large machine for its time. The Great War extended beyond Europe, and in July 1918, an O/400 flew from England to Egypt to be based in Palestine, and was operated against the Turks.

Nearly 600 Handley Page O/400s were built, including 107 built in America by the Standard Aircraft Corporation.

The O/400 remained in service until late 1919, when it was replaced by the Vickers Vimy. Even then, its lifespan continued, with some being converted for civilian use. Eight were used to transport officials between London and Paris for the negotiations of the Treaty of Versailles.

Fairey Campania

In the latter part of 1914, the Royal Navy purchased an elderly ocean liner called the *Campania*. The plan was to convert it into a seaplane carrier. The unavoidable challenge was that the ship needed to stop each time it was required to hoist a seaplane into the water or to load it on board when it returned. This made the ship vulnerable to attack by U-boats. The Admiralty sought an alternative strategy and by mid-1916, the *Campania* had been fitted with a 200ft (61m) long flight deck, enabling experimental launches to take place.

A specification was issued by the Admiralty for a two-seat patrol and reconnaissance aircraft.

Fairey Aviation's response was a single-engine tractor biplane constructed of wood with a fabric covering. The wings folded rearward for storage and handling. The observer, in the second cockpit, had a Lewis machine gun on a Scarff ring. Two prototypes were produced, the first designated F.16 was powered by a 250hp (190kW) Rolls-Royce Eagle IV engine, while the second prototype, F.17, had a 275hp (205kW) Rolls-Royce Eagle V. The first flight of the F.16 was on 16 February 1917.

Trials proved satisfactory and a production order was placed for 170 machines to be powered by the 260hp (190kW) Sunbeam Maori II engine. The first aircraft in service joined HMS *Campania*, and the name stuck. The Fairey Campanias also served on HMS *Nairana* and HMS *Pegasus*. The original two prototypes were assigned to Scapa Flow from where they were deployed operationally.

A number of Campanias participated in the North Russia Campaign, part of the Allied intervention in the Russian Civil War in August 1918. Aircraft from HMS *Nairana* took part in a fully combined land, sea and air operation, joining ground forces and ships in driving Bolsheviks out of their stronghold on an island in the mouth of the Northern Dvina River in Russia. The aircraft then scouted ahead up the channel to Archangel. Here the arrival of Campanias overhead caused the Bolshevik leaders to flee in panic.

The Fairey Campania was declared obsolete in August 1919. Only 62 had been built.

The Campania had a top speed of 85mph (137km/h) and a service ceiling of 6,000ft (1,800m). It took seven minutes to reach 2,000ft (610m). The unfolded wingspan was 61ft 7in (18.77m) and its length was 43ft 1in (13.13m).

The Fairey Campania was named after an ocean liner. (Philip Jarrett via Key Archives)

Armstrong Whitworth F.K.8

The F.K.8 was manufactured by Armstrong-Whitworth Ltd of Newcastle-on-Tyne, and designed by Frederick Koolhoven of Holland. It was a more robust and larger aircraft than the Armstrong Whitworth F.K.3. The F.K.3 had been nicknamed the 'Little Ack' by aircrew, so it was inevitable that the F.K.8 would be called the 'Big Ack'.

Fitted with a 120hp (89kW) Beardmore engine, it had a top speed of 83.5mph (134km/h), although later versions had a 160hp (119kW) Beardmore, giving a top speed of 95mph (152km/h). Both engines were water cooled. The F.K.8 was designed and deployed as a two-seat reconnaissance aeroplane. The observer's cockpit was equipped with dual controls to allow the possibility of a crash landing if the pilot became incapacitated.

The F.K.8 was a conventionally constructed aircraft made of wood and fabric. With the 120hp (89kW) motor, the wingspan was 42ft 5in (12.94m), and the length was 29ft 9in (9.07m). With the 160hp (119kW) motor, these increased to a span of 43ft 4in (13.21m) and a length of 31ft 5in (9.59m).

It first flew in May 1916 and was well received in trials, resulting in an initial order for 50 aircraft. When the F.K.8 arrived on the Western Front in early 1917 it provided a welcome replacement for the B.E.2s and R.E.8s, which were increasingly unpopular with aircrew. Even so, there were teething problems, such as the undercarriage not being up to the rough nature of frontline airfields and the usage necessitated by war operations. There were also changes made to the gun synchronisation gear and modifications to the rudder and shape of the fin.

On 30 April 1917, to solve the undercarriage service problems, instructions were issued to replace the undercarriage assemblies with a simplified 'V' form assembly like the Bristol Fighters. Inevitably, this resulted in a temporary shortage for the Bristol Fighter production line and the practice was terminated until May 1918. During the service life of the F.K.8 further changes were made to the shape of the nose cowling and the radiators.

It was produced in large numbers, with 1,650 of the two versions being built. F.K.8s served in France, Palestine and Macedonia but the type was obsolete late in the war and was quickly withdrawn at the end of hostilities. The last squadron to use it was based in Greece and the aircraft were withdrawn in September 1919.

The Armstrong Whitworth F.K.8. (Picryl)

Armament was a single fixed Vickers machine gun synchronised to fire through the propeller arc and a free Lewis machine gun on a Scarff mounting for the observer. The aircraft could also be used for light bombing missions with a variety of bombs held on underwing racks.

Two F.K.8 pilots were awarded the Victoria Cross for gallantry, Second Lieutenant Alan McLeod, RFC, and Captain Ferdinand West of the RAF. Alan McLeod was flying an F.K.8 over Albert, France, when attacked by nine enemy triplanes. By skilful flying, McLeod manoeuvred his aircraft enabling himself and his observer to shoot down four of the enemy. Both airmen were injured, the fuel tank was punctured and the aircraft set alight. McLeod side-slipped, but flames were scorching him so he jumped onto the left wing, crouched and grasped the joystick in his right hand. He smashed a hole through the fabric so he could operate the rudder with his left hand. He guided the aircraft towards the Allied lines, keeping the flames away from his observer. The aircraft finally crashed in No-Man's Land, where McLeod dragged his observer to safety.

Ferdinand West was on a reconnaissance mission in August 1918 to determine enemy positions prior to a major offensive. He spotted enemy activity through a hole in the mist, but was attacked by seven enemy fighters. He was hit in the leg and the radio was wrecked. He continued to record the activity on the ground while manoeuvring the F.K.8 to allow his observer to fire at the enemy aircraft, which flew away. Having completed observation of the German concentration he headed back towards the British lines, twisting his trouser leg into a tourniquet to stem the blood flow from his wounds. He managed to land behind Allied lines and report his findings. The wounds in his left leg had fractured the femur and severed the femoral artery, resulting in amputation.

In addition to the RFC and RAF, military users of the F.K.8 included the Paraguayan Army and the Kingdom of Hejaz Air Force (now part of Saudi Arabia), which received two F.K.8s in 1921, with one still in use in 1923.

The 'Big Ack' gave splendid service during the Great War. (Picryl, public domain)

Wight Converted Seaplane

This 'conversion' was a development from an unsuccessful bomber design. The aircraft was designed and built by John Samuel White and Company Ltd, known as Wight Aircraft and based at Cowes on the Isle of Wight. It had its first flight in 1916.

A total of 50 aircraft were ordered for the RNAS. The initial production aircraft were powered by the 322hp (240kW) Rolls-Royce Eagle IV engines, but a shortage of these meant that later aircraft were fitted with 265hp (198kW) Sunbeam Maori engines.

The Wight Converted Seaplane entered service with the RNAS in 1917 and operated from bases on the south coast of England and from Cherbourg in France. It was from here on 18 August 1917 that a Converted Seaplane bombed and sank a German U-boat, UB-32, with a single 100lb (45kg) bomb.

Although 50 Wight Converted Seaplanes had been ordered, only 37 were constructed. When the Great War ended, there were seven still in service with the RAF. With the Rolls-Royce Eagle engine, the maximum speed was 84mph (135km/h) with a service ceiling of 9,600ft (2,900m) and an endurance of three hours 30 minutes. The wingspan was 65ft 6in (19.96m) and its length was 44ft 8.5in (13.63m).

A Wight Converted Seaplane. (Johan Visschenijk, 1000aircraftphotos.com)

Airco DH4

The DH4 was designed by Geoffrey de Havilland and built by the Aircraft Manufacturing Company in Hendon, London. Despite receiving the nickname 'Flaming Coffin', the DH4 is believed to have been the finest day bomber used in the Great War. It was the first British bomber to have the capability to defend itself.

The nickname was earned due to its reputation for catching fire at the most awkward moments. Even so, its performance, and particularly its service ceiling, made it popular with aircrew and efficient in bombing operations. The fire hazard was largely dealt with later in 1917 by replacing the pressurised fuel tanks with wind-driven fuel pumps.

The prototype DH4 had its first flight in August 1916. Evaluation was carried out at the Central Flying School with good results, and particular praise was given to its time-to-altitude figures, which were unmatched by other aircraft. During late 1916, the RFC placed orders for production of the DH4, as did the RNAS.

Several alternative powerplants were fitted to DH4s. The prototype had used a 230hp (172kW) Beardmore-Halford-Pullinger (BHP) engine, and although performance was viewed as excellent, there was concern over the potential of the BHP motor for production. Consequently, the initial RFC orders for the DH4 meant the aircraft would be powered by Rolls-Royce Eagle III engines of 250hp (186kW). As production increased and development of the Eagle motor produced results, DH4 aircraft were fitted with higher power units culminating in the Eagle VIII of 375hp (280kW).

The DH4 wings were a wood and fabric construction, but the fuselage had plywood engine bearers and plywood covering to just behind the observer's cockpit, with fabric covering from that point. The DH4's wingspan was 42ft 6in (12.95m) and the length was 30ft 8in (9.38m), although the length reduced to 30ft (9.14m) when fitted with the Eagle VIII motor.

The performance figures for the DH4 illustrate the improvements generated by the increased power. With the Eagle III, the aircraft's top speed was 117mph (187km/h) and its service ceiling 18,000ft (5,486m). The Eagle VIII gave a top speed of 136.5mph (218km/h) and a service ceiling of 22,000ft (6,705m). This remarkable performance meant that the DH4 was able to evade most German fighters if it crossed the lines at its ceiling, and all but the fastest of them on its way home.

However, in a fight with an enemy aircraft, the DH4 had a weakness. Although the pilot had a fixed Vickers machine gun with Constantinesco hydraulic synchronisation to fire through the propeller arc, and the observer had either single or twin Lewis machine guns on a Scarff ring, the distance between the front and rear cockpits meant there was virtually no communication between them. This created difficulty in enabling the pilot to position the DH4 to enable the observer to attack the enemy aircraft, seriously hindering the fighting efficiency.

The DH4 was issued to a home-based squadron, which then proceeded to the Western Front in March 1917. During spring 1917, the RNAS also received DH4s. In addition to Airco, the DH4 was manufactured by a variety of sub-contractors including F.W. Berwick and Co, Glendower Aircraft Company, Palladium Autocars, Vulcan Motor and Engineering and Westland Aircraft. Later in 1917, demand for the aircraft accelerated as retaliatory bombing raids on German facilities followed the German Gotha attacks on Britain.

Not surprisingly, modifications and changes were made as production continued. A range of engines were fitted to the DH4. Although the production aircraft were by now being fitted with the 375hp (280kW) Rolls-Royce Eagle VIII engine, by January 1917 there was a shortage of Rolls-Royce engines, and those from Beardmore-Halford-Pullinger, the Royal Aircraft Factory, Siddeley and Fiat were tried, but none gave the DH4 the performance of the Rolls-Royce engine.

Despite its nickname 'Flaming Coffin', the Airco DH4 was a very successful aircraft. (Picryl)

Successful attacks were made on munition factories in Mannheim, Metz-Sablon, Frankfurt and Stuttgart, a daring RNAS attack was made on the Zeebrugge mole. From the spring of 1918, the number of DH4s in frontline service began to decline as engine shortages continued and aircraft production switched to the De Havilland DH9.

When the US entered the Great War, the United States Army Air Force did not have aircraft suitable for frontline service. The DH4, along with the Bristol Fighter, were selected as suitable machines for US military use. The first American-built DH4 was sent to France in May 1918 and commenced operations in August. The American aircraft differed from the British version in the type of engine and the synchronisation gear. The 400hp (300kW) Liberty L-12 motor was fitted and the aircraft had two forward-firing 0.30in (7.62mm) Martin-Rockwell machine guns in the nose and two Lewis machine guns in the rear cockpit. Of the six Medals of Honor awarded to US airmen in the Great War, four were awarded to DH4 crew.

Of the 6,295 DH4s manufactured, 4,846 were built in the US.

At the end of the war, 1,170 DH4s were in service with the RAF, 18 in the Middle East, 664 in France with the RAF, 67 with the Dover-Dunkirk Command, 91 with the Independent Air Force (a strategic bombing force set up to undertake actions with the need to co-ordinate with the army, navy and air force), and the remainder with training units.

American-built DH4s were scrapped by burning at the end of the war rather than by being shipped home. However, there were many in the US that had never shipped to France. These continued to serve with the United States Army Air Corps, the United States Navy and the United States Marine Corps until as late as 1932.

After the Armistice, the RAF formed a communication squadron equipped with DH4s to convey important passengers to and from the Paris Peace Conference. Several were modified to have an enclosed cabin for two passengers.

Airco DH5

Built by the Aircraft Manufacturing Company Ltd (Airco) in Hendon, the DH5 was an extremely unusual design by Geoffrey de Havilland. Its wings were in a reverse stagger form, with the upper wing set 27in (0.69m) behind the lower wing. There was logic to this. The aircraft was intended as a replacement for the 'pusher' format fighters, particularly perhaps the DH2, which had been deployed to the RFC and RNAS as a response to the Fokker Eindekker with its synchronised fire power, for which at that time the Allies had no answer.

By moving the top wing back, it was expected that the benefits of a tractor aircraft could be matched to the superior visibility offered by the pusher layout. In virtually every other way the DH5 construction and powerplant choice was orthodox. It was a wooden structure covered with fabric and the engine was a nine-cylinder Le Rhone rotary unit delivering 110hp (82kW). This gave the aircraft a maximum speed of 102mph (163km/h) and an endurance of two hours 45 minutes.

The wings of the DH5 had two spruce main spars with lattice secondary ribs, and were fabric covered. The forward section of the fuselage was spruce covered with plywood, but the area behind the rear centre section struts was made of wood with a fabric covering. The wingspan was 25ft 8in (7.82m), and the length of the aircraft was 22ft 4in (6.81m). To maintain the centre of gravity given the shift forward of the pilot and rearward for the upper wing, the fuel tank was situated behind the pilot's cockpit although an auxiliary tank was fitted above the upper wing and slightly offset to the right. This provided gravity feed to the engine.

Armament came in the form of a single Vickers machine gun, synchronised for the propeller arc and fitted above and slightly to the right of the pilot's cockpit. Both telescopic and ring and bead sights were fitted. Many considered the DH5 to be under-armed in having a single machine gun.

The Airco DH5 was Geoffrey de Havilland's attempt to marry the benefits of a tractor engine layout with the pilot's visibility in a pusher engine. (Picryl)

The first prototype was subjected to tests by the manufacturer in late 1916. These resulted in the fitting of enlarged fin and rudder assemblies to improve directional control. On 9 December, the prototype began service trials with the Central Flying School at Upavon in Wiltshire. Although generally favourable, criticism focused on the poor rear view and disappointing performance, which other aircraft could already exceed.

Even so, in January 1917, orders were issued for an initial 400 DH5s. Modification continued to be made prior to production, with a revised fuselage and structural changes, and use of plywood provided great strength but added complexity.

The first significant batches of DH5s arrived in France in July 1917. They were primarily used for escort patrols with Sopwith Pups. Because the Pups were capable of holding their ceiling better than the DH5s, the DH aircraft patrolled the lower levels of the formation. The unobstructed view forward and the ability to withstand the pressure of long dives meant that the DH5 was ideal for ground-strafing missions, which were almost suicidal patrols. It served well in the ground-attack role during the Battle of Cambrai from 20 November to 7 December 1917.

The DH5 did not become popular with pilots, mainly because it was considered a dangerous aircraft to land. Of Geoffrey de Havilland's wartime designs, the DH5 was considered the least successful. There seems to have been some substance to the concern about landing. The back stagger created a loss of aerodynamic efficiency due to turbulence between the upper and lower wings, leading to poor control when approaching the stall. As a result, there were many accidents during training.

Nevertheless, a total of 483 DH5 scouts were built of which 340 reached the Western Front in 1917 and 140 were issued to training units. The final DH5s were replaced by the S.E.5A in January 1918.

In addition to the RFC, the Australian Flying Corps also used the DH5.

An Airco DH5 displays the back stagger of its wings. (Alamy)

Felixstowe 2A Flying Boat

The design of the Felixstowe 2A was mainly the work of Lieutenant Commander John Porte, who retired from the Royal Navy prior to the outbreak of the Great War. He had helped the American aircraft designer, Glenn Curtiss, to develop the Curtiss H12 flying boat, which had been used by the RNAS. When war broke out, Lieutenant Commander Porte took a commission in the RNAS. His immediate recommendation was to buy the Curtiss H-4 flying boat with which he was familiar, having worked on it in the US. The RNAS duly acquired two Curtiss Americas, a forerunner of the H-4, and 62 Curtiss H-4 flying boats. They were not a success, being considered underpowered, having a weak hull and poor handling characteristics whether afloat or at take-off. One commentator said that they were nose-heavy with the engines underpowered, and that it was tail-heavy when gliding.

John Porte conducted experiments with the Curtiss machine using different hulls, calling on his experience and knowledge to modify and develop the Curtiss basic design. The result was a hull with a length of 36ft (11m), which was fitted to the wings and tail unit of a Curtiss H-4. The aircraft was fitted with twin 150hp (112kW) Hispano-Suiza 8 engines. The resulting machine was called the Felixstowe F.1.

The hull was built around a sturdy wooden box girder, which gave the strength that was lacking in earlier designs. The initial single-step hull bottom was modified by the addition of two more steps. The resulting hull proved more seaworthy and gave better take-off and landing characteristics.

Having proved the concept, Porte married the new design of the hull to the larger Curtiss H-12 flying boat's wings and tail, adding two 345hp (257kW) Rolls-Royce Eagle VIII engines. This aircraft was

A Felixstowe F.2A flying boat painted in bizarre fashion to assist its recovery in the event of ditching. (Picryl)

named the Felixstowe F.2. The aircraft went into production as the Felixstowe F.2A. The wingspan was 95ft 7½in (29.14m) and the length was 46ft 3in (14.1m). The Felixstowe 2A had a maximum speed of 95mph (152km/h), a service ceiling of 9,500ft (2,895m) and an endurance of up to seven hours.

The 2A was fitted with twin Lewis machine guns in the cockpit and behind the wings, mounted on Scarff rings. Side gun positions were also mounted on some aircraft. A medium bombload of up to 460lb (210kg) could be carried externally on racks beneath the wings. The bomb load was capable of destroying a submarine even if a direct hit was not achieved.

The Felixstowe 2A entered service in 1917 as a reconnaissance and anti-submarine flying boat. The manufacturer was Short Bros of Rochester, Kent, although sub-contractors were also used including S.E. Saunders Ltd of the Isle of Wight, which built 100 Felixstowe F.2As. The early aircraft had fabric covering to the upper section of the hull, but this was replaced on later aircraft with plywood planking. About 100 were built before the Great War ended, but another 73 were constructed after the conflict.

The 2As were based at seaplane stations all around the British coast. In October 1918, there were 53 Felixstowe 2As with the RNAS. They were used for attacking Zeppelins on reconnaissance over the North Sea as well as duties with hydrophones.

One weakness was the fuel transfer system in which fuel had to be pumped from the tank in the hull to the motors. There were many cases when the aircraft were forced down onto the sea through fuel-feed problems rather than enemy action. To aid rescue, Yarmouth-based aircraft were painted with bizarre colour schemes chosen by the individual crews, but at Great Yarmouth a standardised colour scheme was adopted.

The Felixstowe F3 was a larger and heavier version of the 2A, but although its bombload was greater, the aircraft lost agility compared to its smaller sibling. In total, 100 were built before the end of the war, of which 18 were constructed in Malta.

Airco DH9

Another Geoffrey de Havilland design, manufactured by the Aircraft Manufacturing Company Ltd, the DH9 was aptly described by some as a DH4 that had been officially interfered with to make it suitable for mass production, powered by the Beardmore-Halford-Pullinger engine. The main modifications to the basic DH4 design were the repositioning of the pilot's cockpit behind the centre section to be closer to the observer, and the only partially cowled engine. Moving the cockpits also meant the fuel tank was further away from the pilot, a point of concern with the DH4. As a result of the repositioning of the pilot, the DH9 was considered unsuitable for night bombing due to visibility limitations.

It was against a background of German attacks on London that in July 1917, on a recommendation from the War Office, the British Cabinet approved a virtual doubling in size of the RFC with the expectation that the new squadrons proposed should be primarily bomber squadrons. At about the same time, drawings of a replacement for the DH4 were presented, which offered increased range and the prospect of a completely new engine, which would provide a performance to match enemy fighters.

Thus was born the DH9. Even before its first flight, orders for more than 4,600 aircraft were placed. Some contracts for the DH4 were changed to the DH9. It was a fairly standard construction made of wood and fabric, except that the front part of the fuselage back to the rear cockpit was plywood covered. The aircraft could carry a radio and camera. The wingspan was 42ft 6in (12.95m), and the length 30ft 9½in (9.38m).

The new engine was the Beardmore-Halford Pullinger (BHP) Galloway Adriatic motor on which much depended; with its predicted 300hp (220kW). The first prototype, actually a converted DH4, had its first flight in July 1917. Exhaustive tests followed, which showed that the BHP engine was incapable of reliably delivering its expected power and had been de-rated to 230hp (170kW) in order to improve its reliability. The dramatic effect on performance meant that the DH9 was in this respect inferior to the DH4 it was intended to replace.

The Airco DH9. (Picryl)

The effect on performance meant that, unlike the DH4, the DH9 would, of necessity, have to fight its path through enemy fighters with superior performance. In November 1917, deliveries to the RFC began. Some senior officials raised objections to the deployment of the aircraft but President of the Air Council Sir William Weir said that it was a matter of having the DH9 or nothing at all. In any event, production was already well under way.

The DH9 was armed with a single fixed Vickers machine gun synchronised to fire through the propeller arc, and a single Lewis machine gun for the observer, although later models had twin-yoked Lewis guns in this position.

Bombing formations of DH9s were often reduced in strength before they crossed the lines because the motors of some machines would not develop sufficient power to enable the aircraft to maintain station. Even worse, the DH9s could not maintain their height at 15,000ft (4,572m) with a full bomb load, and were often forced to descend, making them even more vulnerable.

The volume of production meant that sub-contractors were needed, and many DH9s were built by companies such as Alliance, G & J Weir, Short Brothers, Vulcan, Waring and Gillow and National Aircraft Factories.

Losses of DH9 aircraft over the Western Front were very high, as predicted. Between May and the Armistice in November 1918, two squadrons lost 54 DH9s shot down and a further 94 were written off because of accidents. Even so, the DH9 did a huge amount of strategic bombing over the Rhine, continuing until the Armistice. There were also instances of real accomplishment. On 9 August 1918, a DH9 on a bombing mission shot down four enemy fighters that were attacking the DH9 formation, and on 23 August, it is believed that another DH9 flown by Lieutenant A.R. Spurling with his observer Sergeant F. Bell single-handedly attacked a superior number of Fokker DVIIs and accounted for several of them.

The DH9 was also deployed in the Middle East where it had more success against Turkish forces, probably because the quality of the opposing aircraft was poorer.

Although a variety of engines were tried in the aircraft, it was not until the Rolls-Royce Eagle or the American Liberty motors were available that the DH9 finally emerged as the DH9A. A total of 2,166 DH9s were built, 92 seeing service in the Middle East and 52 being used for anti-submarine patrols.

The DH9 was finally withdrawn by the RFC in 1920. Its final combat mission took place in Somalia in January and February 1920.

Military users of the DH9 included the Afghan Air Force, Australian Air Force, Belgian Air Force, Canadian Air Force, Bolivian Air Force, Chilean Air Force, Estonian Air Force (1919–33), Indian Air Force, Royal Hellenic Naval Service, Hejaz Air Force, Irish Air Service, Latvian Air Force, Royal Netherlands East Indies Army Air Force, New Zealand Air Force, Paraguayan Air Force, Peruvian Air Force, Polish Air Force (1920–29), Royal Romanian Air Force, Spanish Air Force, South African Air Force, Soviet Air Force, Swiss Air Force, Turkish Air Force, American Expeditionary Force, United States Marine Corps and Uruguayan Air Force.

Royal Aircraft Factory S.E.5a

The S.E.5 stands alongside the Sopwith Camel as the most famous British fighter/scout of the Great War. It was a product of the Royal Aircraft Factory, and by far its best design. It was also built by subcontractors including Vickers Ltd, Martin and Handasyde and the motor car manufacturers Austin and Standard.

Gone was the air-cooled rotary motor. In its place was a variety of Hispano-Suiza motors, 150hp (112kW) for the S.E.5 and 200, 220, 240hp, (149, 164 or 179kW) Hispano-Suizas, or a 200hp (149kW) Wolseley Viper motor for the S.E.5a. With the Viper motor, the S.E.5a had a top speed of 132mph (211km/h) and an endurance of two and a half hours.

The design team included Henry Folland and Major Frank Godden of the Royal Aircraft Factory. The first flight of the S.E.5 was on 22 November 1916. Frank Godden was killed when the prototype crashed due to weakness in the wing design. The second prototype was also lost in a crash, but the third underwent modification that resolved the problem.

Although much of the construction was conventional wood and fabric covering, part of the fuselage was covered in plywood, the wing centre section was steel and the engine cowling was made of aluminium. A single fixed Vickers machine gun was situated above the engine cowling, synchronised with the Constantinesco gearing to fire through the propeller arc, and a Lewis machine gun was mounted above the wing centre section, but operated by the pilot via a Bowden cable. The wingspan of the S.E.5 was 28ft (8.53m) and the length was 21ft 4in (6.5m). The S.E.5a had a wingspan of 26ft 7½in (8.11m), and a length of 20ft 11in (6.4m).

Deliveries of the aircraft to frontline squadrons began in April 1917. Until its arrival, the German Albatros fighter had arguably been the supreme aircraft on the Western Front and the S.E.5 arrived too late to prevent the heavy RFC losses in 'Bloody April' during the Battle of Arras. Only 77 of the S.E.5 aircraft were built before it became evident that it was underpowered. With the installation of the 200hp (149kW) engines, the S.E.5a was the redesignated aircraft.

Supplies of the French-built Hispano-Suiza engines lagged airframe production. There were difficulties with the reduction gear and there were instances of the propeller, and sometimes the complete gearbox, separating from the engine in flight. As a result, the 200hp (149kW) Wolseley Viper (itself a licence-built version of the Hispano-Suiza 8a engine) became the standard powerplant for the S.E.5a. More than 5,000 S.E.5a aircraft were built by Austin Motors, Air Navigation and Engineering Co, Curtiss Aeroplane and Motor Co, Martinsyde, the Royal Aircraft Factory, Vickers, and Wolseley Motors Ltd.

The S.E.5a redressed the balance in the air over the Western Front, proving a match for the German fighter. Allied air aces William Avery Bishop, Edward Corringham Mannock and James Thomas McCudden scored most of their victories flying the S.E.5a. James McCudden was an ex-RFC mechanic and he customised his S.E.5a by replacing the pistons with high-compression pistons, shortening the exhaust and changes to the ignition, fuel/air mixture and other engine settings. He increased the top speed by 9mph (15km/h) and raised the service ceiling to 20,000ft (6,096m).

The S.E.5a was much easier to handle in the air than the Sopwith Camel, but lacked the manoeuvrability that the Camel's rotary engine delivered. It was therefore with a mixed reaction that former Camel pilots greeted its replacement with the S.E.5a. Yet, the narrow body enabled an excellent view and the aircraft was structurally strong, enabling high speed, dives to be undertaken without fear of breaking up on recovery. As a stable gun platform and with its high speed, the S.E.5a could open fire at a greater range than many of its peers.

When the US entered the war in April 1917, plans for American production of Allied aircraft already in service were under discussion. Initially 38 S.E.5as built by Austin were assigned to the American Expeditionary Force, and the US government ordered about 1,000 to be built by Curtiss. Although only

British Military Biplanes: 1912–19

A Royal Aircraft Factory S.E.5a displaying its clean lines. (Roger Staker)

one of these had been completed before the end of the war, another 56 were assembled using components that had previously been delivered.

By October 1918, 2,973 S.E.5 and 5a aircraft had been delivered to the RAF. The Western Front squadrons received 1,998 of these during 1917 and 1918. About 200 were used in the Middle East, the remainder going to training units.

Other military users of the S.E.5a included the Argentine Navy, which used one from 1926 to 1929, the Australian Flying Corps, Australian Air Force, Brazilian Army Aviation, Canadian Air Force, Chilean Air Force, Irish Air Force, Polish Air Force, South African Air Force and the United States Navy.

Sopwith F.1 Camel

The Sopwith Camel first appeared on the Western Front in July 1917 in time for the Third Battle of Ypres, better known as Passchendaele. The Camel has become legendary for a number of reasons. Most importantly, it was responsible for destroying more enemy aircraft than any other Allied fighter.

During 1916, it became clear that the Sopwith Pup was outclassed by the newer German Fighters, notably the Albatros D.III. What became the Camel was a fighter developed to replace the Pup with heavier armament and greater speed. The name 'Camel' was never officially sanctioned, but it came from the metal fairing secured over the machine gun breeches to prevent freezing, which gave the aircraft a hump appearance.

The Sopwith Camel was manufactured by the Sopwith Aviation Company at Kingston-on-Thames and by a sub-contractor, Boulton and Paul Ltd in Norwich. Power came from either a 110hp (82kW) Le Rhone rotary engine or a 130hp (97kW) Clerget rotary unit. The Le Rhone gave the Camel a maximum speed of just over 118mph (188km/h), while the Clerget was a little slower at just over 106mph (170km/h). Endurance with either engine was two hours 30 minutes.

The Camel was entirely standard in its wood and fabric construction, with an aluminium engine cowling and some plywood panelling around the cockpit. The wingspan was 28ft (8.53m) and its length was 18ft 8in (5.69m).

Armament for the Camel was a pair of fixed Vickers machine guns synchronised to fire through the propeller arc by a Constantinesco gear, the Camel being the first British fighter to be equipped in this way.

The prototype first flew on 22 December 1916, piloted by Harry Hawker. The British War Office issued the first order for 250 Camels in May 1917 and by the end of that year, 1,325 Camels had been produced.

The Camel was a handful to fly, and undoubtedly caused the death of some novice pilots. This was due to the gyroscopic effect of the relatively short fuselage, sensitive elevators and the powerful rotary engine, which meant that the aircraft spun quickly and could turn very fast in the right-hand direction. In skilled hands, these provided the pilot with unmatched manoeuvrability with which to challenge the enemy, but could readily lead to a loss of control for the newcomer. A stall invariably resulted in a dangerous spin and it is said that RFC pilots joked that the Camel offered a choice between a wooden cross, the Red Cross, or a Victoria Cross.

The Sopwith Camel entered service with the RNAS in June 1917 and on 4 July its first combat mission took place, coupled with a claim for the first Camel victory. Canadian pilot Major William Barker scored most of his 46 victories against enemy aircraft and balloons between September 1917 and September 1918 flying his 'personal' Sopwith Camel. His Camel (no. B6313) became the most successful fighter aircraft in the history of the RAF.

From July 1917, the RNAS flew Camels for home defence operations against the Gotha bombers. Public concern and anger about what they perceived to be the poor defence of London prompted the RFC to divert some Camels to home-defence roles. By August 1918, there were seven squadrons of Camels dedicated to home defence. To counter the move by German bombers and their night-time raids, home-defence Camels were equipped with navigation lights to serve as night fighters. A small number were more extensively modified by moving the pilot's cockpit rearwards and replacing the Vickers machine guns with over-wing Lewis machine guns. This enabled the pilot to reload the guns and to fire them without affecting his night vision. It also enabled the use of incendiary ammunition. These modified Camels were known as Sopwith Comics! Camel night fighters were also used on the Western Front.

The RFC and RNAS merged on 1 April 1918 to form the Royal Air Force (RAF). As chance would have it, only a few weeks later, on 21 April, the newly numbered Squadron 209 was tasked with flying a

The almost legendary Sopwith F.1 Camel fighter. (Roger Staker)

patrol over the Western Front. For the German airmen of Manfred von Richthofen's squadron (Jasta 11) it had been a dismal morning due to fog at the airfield at Cappy. Then the mist started to clear and news came of British aircraft over the front lines, so they took off to intercept. A melee of aircraft, Camels and Fokker Dr1 Triplanes took place. Von Richthofen pursued a Camel at low level, but was himself pursued by a Camel flown by a Canadian, Captain A.R. Brown. Intent on chasing what he thought would be his next victim, Von Richthofen flew low over trenches manned by Australian troops who fired at the red Fokker. The Triplane crash-landed and the Red Baron was dead. Although it now seems likely that the fatal shot was fired from the ground rather than from the air – both guns used .303 ammunition – there is no doubt that the Sopwith Camel played a part in the Red Baron's demise.

By mid-1918, the Camel had been outclassed as a day fighter by the Fokker DVII. However, it remained viable as a ground-attack aircraft and was successfully deployed in this capacity during the German spring offensive of March 1918.

From its introduction to the RFC in July 1917 to the Armistice in November 1918, RFC Camels destroyed 908 enemy aircraft. In addition, Camel 2F.1s of the RNAS (see below) destroyed another 373 enemy machines. A total of 4,188 Camels of all variants had seen service by November 1918 with the RAF. At that time on the Western Front, there were 616 in squadron service, another 274 were in the Middle East, 376 were on Home Defence and 1,379 were allocated to training units.

The Camel saw further combat action in Russia as part of British intervention in the Russian Civil War during 1919 and the beginning of 1920, supporting Royal Navy ships and White Russian forces.

In addition to the RFC and RNAS, Camels were used by the Australian Flying Corps, Belgian Aviation Militaire Belge and Groupe de Chasse, Canadian Air Force, French Government, Estonian Air Force, Georgian Air Force, Hellenic Navy, Latvian Air Force, Royal Netherlands Air Force, Polish Air Force (1921), Imperial Russian Air Force, Soviet Air Force, American Expeditionary Force, United States Army Air Force and United States Navy.

Sopwith 2F.1 Camel

The airframe of the Camel 2F.1 was almost identical to the F.1. However, the 2F.1 was operated by the RNAS as well as the RFC. This version of the Camel was equipped with either a 150hp (112kW) Bentley B.R.1 rotary engine or a 230hp (172kW) Bentley B.R.2 rotary powerplant. With the B.R.1, maximum speed was 115mph (184km/h), and with the B.R.2 it rose to 121mph (194km/h). Again, endurance was two hours 30 minutes.

The RNAS aircraft had a single fixed Vickers machine gun and a Lewis machine gun mounted on the upper wing centre section. The shipboard Camels had the fuselage section behind the cockpit, which was capable of being detached for storage.

In November 1918, there were 514 'Bentley'-engined Camels still on charge, of which 210 were on the Western Front, 84 were in store and 129 were operating from aircraft carriers or from lighters towed by destroyers. In August 1918, a Bentley Camel intercepted and destroyed a Zeppelin (L.53) at 19,000ft (5,790m) in the Heligoland Bight. Experimental Camels were also used for dive bombing and for the possible escorting of airships.

A Sopwith 2F.1 Camel takes off from a carrier. Note the Lewis machine gun on the upper wing centre section. (Alamy)

Short Type 320

In 1916, the RNAS sought a seaplane to carry the new Mark IX torpedo. Short Bros, an accomplished manufacturer of seaplanes with the Admiralty Type S.184, responded to the requirement with a design that was larger than the S.184, but typical of the basic design.

The first two prototypes were powered by a single 310hp (231kW) Sunbeam Cossack engine and were designated the Short Type 310. When production was undertaken, the aircraft were powered by a 320hp (239kW) Sunbeam Cossack engine, and the designation '320' stuck.

In addition to designing what would become the 320 torpedo bomber, Short's developed a similar aircraft as a patrol seaplane. It used the same fuselage and powerplant, but wings of equal span rather than the unequal span of the torpedo bomber. Two prototype patrol seaplanes were ordered.

The first torpedo bomber was completed in July 1916, and the second aircraft in August. They were immediately sent to the Adriatic.

The first prototype patrol seaplane was tested in September 1916 but was not considered a sufficient improvement over the S.184 to justify production, and this proposal was dropped. The second of these aircraft was completed as a torpedo bomber.

A Short Type 320 launches a torpedo. (Picryl)

The torpedo bomber had its limitations. The aircraft was flown from the rear cockpit, the front cockpit being occupied by the observer. When the observer needed to use the machine gun, which was level with the top wing, he had to stand on the fuselage coaming. In addition, the aircraft could not carry the torpedo and the observer at the same time.

In early 1917, orders for 25 torpedo bombers were placed and the first examples were delivered to the RNAS in Italy. As a result of two accidents where fuselage collapse followed torpedo release, changes to the fuselage securing wires were made. There was an inevitable delay in using the aircraft in operations.

In September 1917, the first operation using the Type 320 was carried out. Six aircraft were towed on rafts to a position south of Traste Bay, Montenegro. The plan was to attack enemy submarines that were lying off Kotor. The aircraft had to be towed into position because they could not carry enough fuel for the operation in addition to the torpedo. Strong winds and high seas prevented two aircraft from taking off and the mission was abandoned. On the return journey, one aircraft was lost and the others damaged.

Although a few Type 320 machines were used in the UK for experimental purposes during 1918, the remainder were deployed as reconnaissance seaplanes until the end of the war. It is believed that the Type 320 torpedo bomber never dropped a torpedo in anger. The only overseas user of the Type 320 was the Japanese Imperial Navy, which acquired a single example. Total production was 127 examples.

The 320 had a length of 45ft 9in (13.94m). The upper wingspan was 75ft (22.86m), while the lower wingspan was 46ft 9½in (14.26m).

The Short Type 320 on a training flight. (Picryl, public domain)

Beardmore W.B.III

William Beardmore and Company was an engineering and shipbuilding company that had opened an aviation department. Like many companies during the Great War, William Beardmore built aircraft under licence, including the Royal Aircraft Factory B.E.2c and the Sopwith Pup and Camel.

The W.B.III was the company's most successful design, based on the Sopwith Pup. Beardmore's aircraft was extensively modified and adapted especially as a single-seat shipboard fighter. It had redesigned wings with no stagger and an extra set of struts, which enabled folding for storage and handling on board the ship. The modified fuselage had emergency flotation gear.

In February 1917, the prototype received acceptance from the RNAS and 100 production aircraft were ordered. The first 13 W.B.IIIs had folding undercarriages, but the next production run of aircraft had undercarriages that could be jettisoned. The aircraft were armed with a single Lewis machine gun. Power was provided by either a Clerget or Le Rhone rotary engine, both of 80hp (60kW).

The Beardmore W.B.III was deployed on the aircraft carriers HMS *Furious* and HMS *Argus*, and on HMS *Nairana* and HMS *Pegasus*, which were seaplane tenders.

The maximum speed was 103mph (166km/h) and its service ceiling was 12,400ft (3,800m). The wingspan was 25ft (7.6m) and its length was 20ft 3in (6.17m).

The Beardmore W.B.111 naval fighter. (Picryl)

Norman Thompson N.T.2B

Towards the end of 1916, the Norman Thompson Flight Company made a proposal to the Admiralty for the development of a flying boat training aircraft to facilitate the training of pilots for the larger flying boats, such as the Felixstowe F.2 and the Curtiss Americas. The proposal was accepted and in November 1916 an order for ten aircraft was placed for the RNAS.

The aircraft that was built was the Norman Thompson N.T.2B, a pusher biplane with an enclosed cockpit with side-by-side seating for trainee and instructor with dual controls. It was powered by a 160hp (119kW) Beardmore engine mounted between the wings.

The N.T.2B was ordered into production. Some of the first 50 aircraft had 150hp (112kW) Hispano-Suiza engines, but the later aircraft were fitted with 200hp (149kW) Sunbeam Arab engines. When these proved to be unreliable, the engine choice changed to the 200hp (149kW) Hispano-Suiza 8 engine.

The demand for the N.T.2B exceeded the capacity of Norman Thompson to build and deliver, and Supermarine and S.E. Saunders of Cowes were sub-contracted to support the production. By the end of the Great War, it is estimated that nearly 300 aircraft had been ordered, but cancellations following the Armistice meant that only 150 were actually built.

First deliveries were made to the RNAS on 8 July 1917, and it became the standard flying boat trainer aircraft. Following the end of the war, N.T.2B aircraft were sold to the air forces of Canada, Estonia, Norway and Peru as well as the Imperial Japanese Navy.

With the 200hp (149kW) Sunbeam Arab engine, it had a top speed of 85mph (137km/h) and a service ceiling of 11,400ft (3,500m). The wingspan was 48ft 4¾in (14.75m) and its length was 27ft 4½in (8.34m).

A Norman Thompson N.T.2B flying boat trainer aircraft. (Ron D. Myers, 1000aircraftphotos.com)

Norman Thompson N.T.4

In 1912, Norman Thompson and Douglas White formed a company to design and build aircraft. In September 1915, the company became the Norman Thompson Flight Company.

The first aircraft to be designed and built by the renamed company was the N.T.4, a twin-engine flying boat with 200hp (150kW) Hispano-Suiza engines mounted in pusher configuration. The crew of four were accommodated in a fully glazed cockpit. There was provision for Lewis machine guns to be operated through side windows.

In December 1915, an order for ten aircraft was placed and the first prototype flew in October 1916. In 1917, additional orders brought the number on order to 50, but in 1918 a change in policy by the Admiralty on anti-submarine aircraft resulted in the cancellation of 20. Production continued until June 1918, when a total of 26 had been built.

The N.T.4 was operated in anti-submarine roles over the North Sea and the English Channel and many were used for training. Some of the later aircraft were delivered directly to store and never used.

The maximum speed was 95mph (153km/h) and it had a service ceiling of 11,000ft (3,600m) with an endurance of six hours. The N.T.4s wingspan was 78ft 7in (23.95m) and its length was 41ft 6in (12.65m).

The Norman Thompson N.T.4 anti-submarine flying boat. (Ron D. Myers, 1000aircraftphotos.com)

Pemberton-Billing AD Flying Boat

The AD Flying Boat was a 1915 design by Pemberton-Billing Ltd for a patrol aircraft that could be an asset to the Royal Navy's warships. The company's manager director, Hubert Scott-Paine, was a shrewd businessman and kept in close contact with the Admiralty's Air Department to understand its requirements and how best to respond. 'AD' in the name of the flying boat stands for Admiralty Department.

The AD Flying Boat was a conventional aircraft with the pilot and observer seated in tandem in the nose of the aircraft, with the single engine being mounted in a pusher configuration behind them. The wings could be folded for storage and handling on board ship. Two prototypes were built. Although it was intended that the first prototype would be powered by a 150hp (112kW) Sunbeam Nubian engine, this was not yet available, so a 200hp (150kW) Hispano-Suiza engine was fitted instead.

The first aircraft had its maiden flight in 1916. In tests, it performed badly, with severe fore and aft vibration during the take-off, and there was a handling problem in flight with excessive yaw being encountered. Changes to the hull as well as the fin and rudder assembly cured the problems, resulting in orders being placed for the AD Flying Boat. Although a total of 80 aircraft were ordered, only 27 were built.

In 1916, Hubert Scott-Paine acquired the company and changed the name to Supermarine Aviation. After the Armistice in 1918, the company re-purchased 19 AD Flying Boats for conversion to civil use under the designation Supermarine Channel. They carried a pilot and three passengers, all in open cockpits. The Channels had some success with both military and civil operators in Chile, Japan, Norway and Sweden.

With a 200hp (150kW) Hispano-Suiza engine, the Flying Boat had a top speed of 100mph (160km/h) and a service ceiling of 11,000ft (3,400m). It carried a single Lewis machine gun and was capable of carrying a small bomb load. The wingspan was 50ft 4in (15.34m) and its length was 30ft 7in (9.32m).

The Pemberton-Billing AD Flying Boat was not a success. (Alamy)

Felixstowe F5

Building on the success of the Felixstowe F2A and the slightly larger F3, John Porte developed a larger flying boat intended to combine the best features and qualities of the F2A and the F3. Compared with the F3, the prototype had a deeper hull and an entirely new wing with a greater span. The power was provided by two 350hp (261kW) Rolls-Royce Eagle VIII engines; these were a slightly uprated version of those fitted in the F3.

The prototype had its first flight in November 1917 and it proved positive. The aircraft showed superior qualities to its predecessors. Testing demonstrated greatly improved performance compared with the F2A and the F3.

The Felixstowe F5 was ordered into production, but unfortunately financial considerations came into play. These resulted in the prototype F5 hull being retained but married to the wings of the F3, and as many F3 components as possible were used in the construction. Tests with the Rolls-Royce Eagle VIIIs showed that performance was now inferior to the Felixstowe F3 it was intended to replace. Even worse, supply problems with the Eagle VIII engines meant that some F5 flying boats were delivered with 325hp (242kW) Rolls-Royce Eagle VII engines. With these, the performance was very disappointing.

British production of the F5 was undertaken by at least 12 companies, with the largest production being by Short Brothers and the Phoenix Dynamo Manufacturing Company. A total of 163 F5s were built.

The F5 did not enter service with the RAF until the end of the Great War and saw no operational service. However, it replaced the earlier aircraft and became the RAF's standard flying boat until superseded in 1925. With the 345hp (257kW) Eagle VIII engines the F5 had a top speed of 88mph (142km/h), a service ceiling of 6,800ft (2,073m) and an endurance of seven hours. The wingspan was 103ft 8in (31.6m) and its length was 49ft 3in (15m). Armament comprised four Lewis machine guns, one in the nose and three amidships, together with up to 920lb (417kg) of bombs carried under the wings.

The United States Navy used an American-built version of the F5 called the F5L, which was powered by two Liberty engines. A total of 227 were built and were in use until the late 1920s. The Hiro Naval Arsenal built an improved version of the F5 under licence for the Imperial Japanese Navy, and these were in use from 1922 to 1930. Hiro then built its own version of the F5 called the H1H, which remained in service until 1938.

The Felixstowe F5 flying boat. (Bill Ewing, 1000aircraftphotos.com)

Sopwith Dolphin

Despite the unpopularity generated by the DH5 with its backward staggered wings, in 1917 Sopwith started work on a single-seat fighter with a similar wing layout. It emerged ready for operational service in early 1918. It was called the Sopwith Dolphin. The lower wing was positioned 13in (33cm) forward of the top wing.

In order to maximise visibility for the pilot, the key reason for the backward stagger, the Dolphin went a step further in that the pilot sat with his head through the centre section and above the upper wing. There was therefore an unobstructed view around and above the aircraft for the pilot. The military advantage was obvious, but it did not prove popular with pilots during testing and training as it usually proved fatal if the aircraft turned over on landing, quite a common occurrence in the Great War. Before the Dolphin reached the Western Front, two modifications were made to alleviate this concern. The first was the installation of a crash pylon above the centre section, and the second was the installation of a quick release exit in the side of the cockpit. These certainly helped, but occasional flyers of the Dolphin still viewed the aircraft with some horror at the thought of being sandwiched between the motor and the fuel tank in the event of a crash. As it happened, this fear disappeared over time and the crash pylons were dispensed with on frontline aircraft.

There were, nevertheless, advantages for the pilot. It was a comfortable cockpit, and it was heated by pipes that carried hot water from the engine along the cockpit walls to the radiator blocks, which were side-mounted. The pilot could control the engine temperature by the use of shutters on the front of each radiator core.

The Dolphin was constructed of spruce and fabric for the wings and fuselage with ash and plywood engine bearers. The upper wings were attached to the fuselage by an open steel framework above the cockpit. Wingspan was 32ft 6in (9.91m) and the length 22ft 3in (6.78m).

The first Dolphin prototype was fitted with a 150hp (112kW) Hispano-Suiza 8B engine with a front radiator, much as would be found on a car. It first flew on 23 May 1917. It was sent to the Aeroplane and Armament Experimental Establishment (A&AEE) for trials. On 13 June, it flew to Saint Omer in France for service trials. So unfamiliar was the design that Allied anti-aircraft gunners opened fire on it.

The popular Sopwith Dolphin fighter. (Picryl)

The reports were favourable and orders for 200 Dolphins were placed by the Ministry of Munitions on 28 June from a subcontractor, Hooper & Company, which was a coachbuilder. Shortly afterwards, an order for another 500 was placed with Sopwith and 200 with Darracq Motor Engineering Company. The second, third and fourth prototypes had a variety of modifications to the radiators, fin and rudder until the final configuration was arrived at. Full production of the Dolphin commenced in October 1917 and the aircraft entered service with the RFC in February 1918.

The Dolphin was heavily armed. The pilot had twin fixed Vickers machine guns synchronised with Constantinesco gear to fire through the propeller arc, and there were twin free Lewis machine guns mounted above the centre section, although these were often removed in service as they could swing into the pilot's face. Some Dolphins were fitted with a Lewis gun on each lower wing. They were splayed slightly outwards and it was not possible for the pilot to change the ammunition drums.

The aircraft became popular with those who used it on the Western Front as it was a formidable fighting machine. Its main drawbacks were its relatively heavy controls, the high landing speed and its tendency to stall viciously. In these respects, it resembled the DH5. The ground engineers did not like rigging challenges created by the back stagger.

The production Dolphin was fitted with a 200hp (149kW) Hispano-Suiza water-cooled motor giving a top speed of 131.5mph (210km/h), a service ceiling of 21,000ft (6,400m) and an endurance of two hours 30 minutes. The Hispano-Suiza engine was not without its problems. There were failures caused by insufficient hardening of the metal used for some of the gearing and also persistent lubrication problems. The French priority was also, understandably, to ensure deliveries for its own Société Pour L'Aviation et ses Dérivés (SPAD) fighter aircraft. Things improved in early 1918.

The Dolphin first appeared on the Western Front in January 1918 and was used for both high-altitude offensive patrols and low-level attacks using machine guns and light bombs. The Dolphin's high-altitude capabilities were utilised against the German reconnaissance aircraft, in particular the Rumpler C.VII, which could operate above 20,000ft (6,100m). The use of oxygen equipment for pilots was explored, but abandoned when it was found that the oxygen tanks exploded if struck by a bullet.

By November 1918, a total of 821 Dolphins had been built of which 400 were in service in France, the remainder being mainly in training units or in store. It is claimed that about 1,500 Dolphin airframes were also constructed but never fitted with engines at the time that the Armistice was signed, and were scrapped. The Dolphin was quickly discarded after the Armistice. It was declared obsolete on 1 September 1921.

In addition to the RFC/RAF, military users included the Canadian Air Force, Polish Air Force, Ukrainian Air Force, American Expeditionary Force and United States Army Air Service.

Sopwith Cuckoo T.1

In late 1916, the RNAS required a torpedo bomber. The Admiral of the Fleet, Sir David Beatty, was one of the prime movers because he had plans to attack German ships and bases in harbour. The other driving force behind the Cuckoo was Commodore Murray Sueter who had very similar plans for the German High Seas Fleet and even identified the ships from which torpedo bombers could be launched. In the event, neither of these schemes took place, but the Cuckoo earned its place in aeronautical history as the precursor to the post-Great War torpedo bombers that played such an important role a little over 20 years later.

The requirement was for a single-seat aircraft capable of carrying a 1,000lb (455kg) torpedo and having an endurance of four hours. It seems that Sopwith was approached directly by Commodore Sueter rather than the requirement being subject to wider competition.

Because the Cuckoo would be carrier-based, the wings were hinged to swing backwards, facilitating storage and deck handling. Although designed to take off from an aircraft carrier, and it could do so in just four seconds, there was no provision for arrester gear and hence no expectation that a carrier landing would take place. The aircraft was made of wood with fabric covering throughout. The wingspan was 45ft 9in (13.94m) and the length was 28ft 6in (8.69m).

A Sopwith Cuckoo launches a torpedo. (Picryl)

The prototype first flew in July 1917 and acceptance by the Admiralty resulted in an order for 100 aircraft being placed in August. Deliveries to training establishments began in August 1918, and during the rest of the year additional orders for the Cuckoo were placed, with total orders amounting to 350.

The aircraft were built by sub-contractors; Blackburn Aeroplane and Motor Company of Leeds building 162, Fairfield Engineering producing 50 and Pegler and Company building 20. Neither Fairfield nor Pegler had previous experience of building aircraft and substantial delays were inevitable. Eventually 232 Sopwith Cuckoos had been constructed by the time production ended in 1919, but only 90 had been delivered by the time the Armistice was signed.

The first aircraft was fitted with a 200hp (149kW) Hispano-Suiza motor, but production models had a 220hp (164kW) Sunbeam Arab. This gave the Cuckoo a top speed of 104mph (166km/h), a service ceiling of 12,000ft (3,658m) and an endurance of four hours.

In November 1918, Cuckoos embarked on HMS *Argus*, but the Great War ended before any operational use took place. The Cuckoo was generally popular with pilots, although the Sunbeam Arab engine did give some problems and was replaced in some aircraft by the Wolseley Viper. The type was eventually withdrawn from RAF service in April 1923. The Imperial Japanese Navy Air Service operated six Sopwith Cuckoos.

Blackburn RN Kangaroo

In 1916, Blackburn Aeroplane and Motor Company built a twin-motor seaplane designated the Blackburn G.P. (General Purpose). It had folding wings and could carry bombs or a torpedo. Only two were built.

The Kangaroo was in effect a landplane version of the G.P., designed in recognition of the Air Ministry's changing attitude towards the use of the landplanes rather than seaplanes for anti-submarine and convoy escort work, thus avoiding the limitations of poor sea conditions and the improved performance landplanes offered. The key difference between the G.P. and the Kangaroo being the undercarriage. It was designed as a heavy bomber and anti-submarine patrol aircraft, powered by twin 250hp (186kW) Rolls-Royce Falcon motors. These gave the Kangaroo a top speed of 98mph (157km/h) and a service ceiling of 10,500ft (3,200m).

Despite its size, its construction was a wooden framework with fabric covering for wings, fuselage and tail unit. The wingspan was 74ft 10in (22.95m) and the length was 44ft 2in (13.46m). Its height was 16ft 10in (5.15m).

It was armed with a free ring-mounted Lewis machine gun in the nose, and a similar mounting in the rear cockpit. Its under-wing racks could carry four 230lb (104kg) bombs.

The first prototype was delivered to the A&AEE in January 1918. Tests with this first aircraft revealed some control problems as well as a tendency for twisting of the rear fuselage. These results meant that the initial order of 50 aircraft was reduced to just 20, some of which were already under construction. After the first five aircraft were built, the remaining machines had 285hp (213kW) Rolls-Royce Falcon III engines in place of the earlier Falcon II.

In April 1918, a squadron of Kangaroos was formed for anti-submarine operations. By the Armistice in November, the Kangaroos had flown 600 hours on patrol, sighted and identified 12 U-boats and attacked 11, sinking one and damaging four more. On 28 August, a U-boat was sighted submerged at Runswick Bay on the East Coast of Yorkshire. It was badly damaged by a near miss from a 520lb (240kg) bomb dropped from a Kangaroo and then a destroyer completed the task.

A total of 20 Kangaroos were built. As the war came to an end only 14 Kangaroos were in service, ten of these with the East Coast Sea Patrol unit. After the war, most of the Kangaroos were converted for civilian use, some modified to take eight passengers. The last RAF Kangaroo was withdrawn in 1929. In addition to the RAF, the only military user was the Peruvian Army Flying Service.

The Blackburn Kangaroo anti-submarine aircraft. (Picryl)

Airco DH9A

Built by the Aircraft Manufacturing Company of Hendon and also Westland Aircraft Ltd of Yeovil, the DH9A was a most welcome replacement for the troublesome and widely disliked DH9. Had it been introduced earlier in the war it might have been a game changer as a two-seat day bomber capable of long-range strategic bombing operations. Potentially these could have covered bombing missions over the whole of Germany, operating from bases in France.

As Airco was heavily committed to other projects such as the DH10 Amiens, the detailed design and development of the first prototype DH9A was carried out by Westland Aircraft as a modification of a DH9, which Westland was building as a sub-contractor. The DH9 wings were lengthened and the fuselage was strengthened.

The chosen engine for the DH9A was the 400hp (298kW) Liberty 12A, as the Rolls-Royce Eagle engines so successfully used in the DH4 were in short supply. The first prototype flew in March 1918. As no Liberty engine was available, it actually flew with a Rolls-Royce Eagle, as did the second prototype, which was built by Airco. They were quickly followed on 19 April by the third prototype with the Liberty engine.

Although the Liberty engine had teething problems, once they were properly understood and resolved, it proved a reliable unit. It gave the DH9A a top speed of 114mph (182km/h), a service ceiling of 16,500ft (5,029m) and an endurance of five hours 45 minutes. The aircraft could carry 107 imperial gallons (485 litres/129 US gallons) of petrol.

The wings were made of spruce spars and ribs, which were fabric covered. The fuselage was an ash structure with spruce stiffeners, the area forward of the rear cockpit was plywood covered, the remainder fabric covered. Its wingspan was 46ft (14m) and its length was 30ft (9.14m).

The Airco DH9A became Britain's standard light bomber. (Picryl)

The DH9A was armed with a fixed Vickers machine gun with Constantinesco gear synchronisation enabling firing through the propeller arc, and either a single or double-yoked Lewis gun(s) on a Scarff ring for the observer. Bomb racks were fitted beneath the lower wings.

The first squadron to receive the new aircraft did so in June 1918, but the aircraft were not transferred to France until the end of August. Even so, it still managed to drop 10.5 tons (9,525kg) of bombs on enemy towns such as Frankfurt, Trier (known as Treves by the English), Koblenz and Mannheim. The aircraft flew in formation using the crossfire to full advantage. There were few losses and it shot down a number of enemy fighters.

At the end of the war, there were 272 DH9As in service. The aircraft continued as Britain's standard light bomber remaining in RAF service until 1931, and was deployed in Russia, the Middle East and India. Nearly 2,000 DH9As were built. In addition, unlicensed production of a copy of the aircraft occurred in Russia with about 2,400 of the type being built, designated R-1. They were seen as the standard light bomber and reconnaissance aircraft by Soviet forces and were used on actions in China and central Asia until late in the 1920s.

Plans to build 4,000 variants of the DH9A in America were thwarted by the end of the Great War and only nine were built. The United States Navy and the United States Marine Corps were both users of the DH9A. Other overseas users included the Afghan Air Force, Australian Air Force, Canadian Air Force, Imperial Iranian Air Force, Latvian Air Force, Mongolian People's Air Force, Portuguese Air Force and Swiss Air Force.

The Airco DH9A was probably the best strategic day bomber of the Great War. (Alamy)

Martinsyde F.4 Buzzard

The Martinsyde Buzzard began life as a private venture by the Martin & Handasyde Company for a high-performance fighter powered by a Rolls-Royce Falcon V-12 engine. The prototype, designated F.3, first flew in or about October 1917. Six aircraft were ordered, the first of these flying in November. During tests, its performance was indeed remarkable, being capable of 142mph (229km/h), resulting in an order for six pre-production and 150 production aircraft. However, all Falcon engines were being earmarked for the Bristol Fighter, and Martin & Handasysde had to rethink the project.

The result was the F.4 Buzzard powered by a 300hp (224kW) Hispano-Suiza 8 motor. Compared with the F.3, the Buzzard had new lower wings and the pilot's cockpit had been moved rearwards. The Buzzard's structure was conventional wood and fabric. The upper wingspan was 32ft 9in (9.98m), and the lower wingspan was 31ft 2.5in (9.52m).

With the new engine, the Buzzard had a top speed of 144.5mph (231km/h) and a service ceiling of 26,000ft (7,925m). This performance made the Buzzard one of the fastest – even possibly the fastest – of any aircraft produced during the Great War. The speed, ease of handling and manoeuvrability resulted in large orders being placed, no less than 1,450 being required. Sub-contractors Boulton & Paul Ltd and Standard Motor Company were brought on board to help with construction.

In addition to the RAF, the French Aeronautique Militaire was a potential user, and 1,500 were planned for the US. Deliveries to the RAF began in July 1918, but only 310 had been delivered when the war ended and only 57 of these would be used. All orders for aircraft which were not under construction were cancelled. Two Buzzards were used as high-speed communications aircraft supporting the British representatives at the 1919 Paris Peace Conference and some were used at the Central Flying School.

Although the RAF did not buy aircraft such as the Buzzard after hostilities ceased, there were some minor export opportunities. The Spanish Air Force acquired 20, Finland 15 and the Soviet Union 41. A handful of Spanish Buzzards were still in service at the beginning of the Spanish Civil War in 1936.

Overseas users of the Buzzard included the Canadian Air Force (a two-seat modification still in use in 1922), Finnish Air Force (still in use in 1940), French Aeronautique Militaire, Irish Air Service, Latvian Air Force, Lithuanian Air Force, Polish Air Force (1923–26), Portuguese Air Force, Spanish Republican Air Force, Spanish Republican Navy, Soviet Air Force, and Escuela Militar de Aeronautica of Uruguay.

The very fast Martinsyde F.4 Buzzard. (via Key Archives)

Handley Page V/1500

RNAS success with night bombing using the Handley Page O/400 encouraged the Air Ministry, in 1917, to adopt a plan to reach further into Germany and to bomb Berlin from bases in East Anglia on the east coast of England. To achieve this required the construction of an even larger bomber than the O/100 or O/400 aircraft. The Air Ministry requirement was for a large night bomber to carry a minimum bomb load of 3,000lb (1,400kg).

Pressure of work at Handley Page and the demands of great security meant that design work took place in Ireland and construction of the prototype was entrusted to Harland and Wolff Ltd of Belfast. This was a closely guarded secret project.

The first aircraft flew on 22 May 1918, but it crashed in June and the second aircraft was not ready until October. Even so, orders for 210 aircraft were placed with Harland and Wolff, Beardmore, Handley Page, Grahame-White and Alliance Aircraft.

Three machines were ready by October 1918 and delivered to the first squadron, based at Bircham Newton in Norfolk. The first bombing mission, to Berlin and then flying on to Prague to re-fuel then onwards to bomb Dusseldorf before returning to base, was scheduled for 8 November.

The Armistice intervened and robbed the RAF of the opportunity to test the benefits of long-range bombing. It would be a little more than another two decades before this would be tested again. The mission was cancelled as technical advice was that the engines on one of the aircraft needed to be changed. This occurred again the next day, although with a different aircraft. As the three aircraft taxied out for the third time to begin the delayed mission, a member of the groundcrew ran out to stop them – the Armistice had been declared.

The V/1500 wings were constructed with wooden spars and ribs, which were fabric covered, and the fuselage was of a similar construction except that there was some plywood covering. This was a large aircraft with a wingspan of 126ft (38.4m), a length of 64ft (19.51m) and it stood 23ft (7.1m) high. It had the capacity for 1,000 Imperial gallons (4,500 litres/1,200 US gallons) of petrol and carried a crew of eight.

The V/1500 was Britain's first four-engine bomber, powered by Rolls-Royce Eagle VIII motors in two nacelles with a tractor motor and a pusher motor in each. Each of the motors had an output of 350hp (261kW), a total sufficient to take the aircraft to 99mph (159k/h) and give it an endurance of 12–14 hours depending on the load.

The Handley Page V/1500 heavy bomber. (Picryl)

The V/1500 was well armed, with a single or twin Lewis machine gun on a Scarff ring in the nose cockpit, which was occupied by the bomb-aimer/navigator, another Lewis gun on a 'rocking-post' mounting in the tail cockpit and a Lewis gun mounted to enable it to fire through a trapdoor beneath the fuselage, to the rear of the wings. A bomb load of 30 250lb bombs was carried internally within the fuselage.

After the Armistice, a V/1500 aircraft made the first flight from England to India via Rome, Malta, Cairo and Baghdad, landing in Cairo on New Year's Day 1919 and arriving in Delhi a few days later. This aircraft was used in a bombing raid on Kabul in the 1920 war against Afghanistan.

With the cessation of hostilities, the large order for V/1500s was reduced and ultimately only about 40 aircraft were completed. Although it is believed construction continued until 1921, the V/1500 was replaced by the Vickers Vimy.

The V/1500 heavy bomber in its compact form for storage. (Picryl, public domain)

Airco DH.10 Amiens

Another heavy bomber arriving late in the day for the Great War was the DH.10 Amiens. It was in response to an Air Board specification, A.2.b, issued in April 1917, which required a day bomber with one or two engines, capable of carrying 500lb (227kg) of bombs, at least two guns with 150lb (68kg) of ammunitions, and the ability to fly at least 110 miles (177km) at 15,000ft (4,572) carrying a full load. Good crew communication was required as well as the ability to remain afloat for a minimum of three hours in the event of a landing in water.

Yet another design by Geoffrey de Havilland, the DH.10 was manufactured by the Aircraft Manufacturing Company with sub-contractor National Aircraft Factory of Heaton Chapel, near Stockport. The DH.10 wings were built from spruce with fabric covering, as was the fuselage except that there was some plywood covering.

When the prototype first flew there was disappointment with the performance. The first flight had been scheduled for January 1918, but actually took place early in March due to labour problems and late delivery of components. The aircraft had been fitted with twin 230hp (170kW) Siddeley Puma engines in 'pusher' mode. The specification had been based on a crew of two, but the prototype had a crew of three. Even so, there was deemed to be sufficient potential for a contract to be issued for a total of four prototypes to be built.

A month later it was subjected to evaluation at the A&AEE where its performance was shown to be well below that required.

It was redesigned around the 360hp (270kW) Rolls-Royce Eagle VIII engines now operating in tractor mode. It demonstrated potential, with a greater bomb load capacity, greater range and a slightly higher top speed than the RAF's best day bomber at that time, the DH9A. It was test flown for two months and convinced Airco that tractor, rather than pusher, configuration was the future direction.

Shortages of the Rolls-Royce Eagle engine prevented production of the DH10 with this powerplant. As a result, the third prototype was fitted with 395hp (295kW) Liberty 12 motors from America, which were in more plentiful supply. This aircraft was damaged in a crash, but was repaired, so it was the

An Airco DH10 Amiens, named after the French city. (Alamy)

fourth prototype that was the subject of final evaluation during August 1918. This was the model for the definitive production aircraft.

The DH10 Amiens was a twin-engine aircraft powered by two 405hp (302kW) Liberty water-cooled in-line engines. These gave a top speed of 117mph (187km/h), a service ceiling of 17,500ft (5,334m) and a six-hour endurance. The wingspan was 64ft 9in (19.74m), almost the same as the length of the Handley Page V/1500, and the length was 39ft 9in (12.12m). The DH10 had a crew of three.

Had the Armistice not occurred, the DH10 would have become the standard day bomber. The military interest was evidenced in the substantial volume of orders placed for the aircraft, at one point exceeding 1,200.

Only eight aircraft had been delivered to the RAF by the Armistice and only a single bombing mission had been undertaken. As a consequence of the end of the war, production was scaled back, but even so more than 250 were built.

Post-war operations were curtailed, but the DH10 saw some interesting service activities. These included bombing assignments in the Third Anglo-Afghan war of 1919. They were used to provide an air mail service to the British Army of Occupation on the Rhine, including a night-time air service to Cologne. A regular air service was operated between Cairo and Baghdad in 1921 until 1923, when the DH10 was finally withdrawn from service.

Although too late for action in the Great War, the DH10 Amiens was a successful post-war bomber. (Alamy)

Sopwith 7F.1 Snipe

The competitive pace of aircraft development by all sides in the conflict meant that the pursuit of new ideas, new technology and new designs was a continuous process. In April 1917, Sopwith's Chief Designer, Herbert Smith, began work on a new fighter to replace the Camel, which was in production and about to enter service. The new aircraft was to be called the Sopwith Snipe.

Sopwith was designing the Snipe as a private venture, having no official sanction, less still a licence, for the development of prototypes. However, Sopwith did have a licence to produce four prototypes of a single-engine bomber called the Rhino, but only two were built. Creative accounting came into play. The first Snipe prototype was completed in October 1917 and was fitted with a 150hp (110kW) Bentley AR.1 rotary engine.

The Snipe's construction was less conventional. The wings were spruce 'I' section main spars and lattice ribs, which were fabric covered. The fuselage had spruce longerons and transverse members, with plywood fairings and stringers to give a streamlined form to the circular section fuselage. All was then fabric covered except for the centre section of the upper wing, which was left uncovered to give better visibility for the pilot.

The second prototype had the more powerful 230hp (172kW) Bentley BR.2 motor and was completed in November 1917. The performance offered by this motor attracted an order for a further four prototypes to be built. The third prototype featured modifications to the wings and a fully circular section to the fuselage. It was evaluated in December when it attained a speed of 119mph (192km/h). It was rebuilt with longer wingspans and submitted for evaluation against Air Ministry Specification A.1(a), which called for a high-altitude single-seat fighter with a top speed of at least 135mph (217km/h) at 15,000ft (4,600m). Additional requirements were a service ceiling of at least 25,000ft (7,600m) while equipped with one swivelling and two fixed machine guns. There was also to be an oxygen supply and heated clothing for the pilot during high-altitude flying.

The Snipe was tested against competitive offerings from Austin, Boulton & Paul and Nieuport, all of them powered by the Bentley BR.2 engine. It seems that there was little difference in performance between the four aircraft, but the Sopwith Snipe was selected and an order for 1,700 aircraft was issued in spring 1918.

The BR.2 motor gave the Snipe a top speed of 121mph (194km/h), a service ceiling of 20,000ft (6,096m) and an endurance of three hours. The Snipe had a wingspan of 30ft 1in (9.2m) and the length was 19ft 9in (6.2m). It was not an especially fast aircraft for 1918 but it had excellent manoeuvrability, was easier to handle than the Camel and had better visibility. Its rate of climb was also superior to the Camel and it had better high-altitude performance. This made it more of a match for the latest German fighters.

The Snipe was the last in the line of fighters powered by rotary engines, but represented this class of aircraft at its very best. Armament was twin fixed Vickers machine guns mounted above the engine cowling in front of the pilot's cockpit and synchronised with the standard Constantinesco gear. There was provision for a Lewis machine gun to be mounted above the centre section but it was not fitted on production aircraft. The Snipe could carry four 25lb (11kg) bombs.

In March 1918, a Sopwith Snipe was subjected to a service evaluation at the Aeroplane Supply Depot at Saint-Omer, France. It reached an altitude of 24,000ft (7,315m) in 45 minutes, but was criticised for being tail-heavy and having a 'poor rudder'.

At the end of August 1918, the first squadron to be equipped with the Snipe received its new aircraft in France, replacing its Sopwith Camel. At the end of October, No. 4 Squadron Australian Flying Corps also received Snipes and was soon in action, claiming 11 victories between 26 and 28 October. The RAF Squadron (No. 43) claimed eight Fokker D.VIIs destroyed on 29 October with the loss of just one Snipe.

Sopwith Snipe was the last rotary engine-powered fighter. (Picryl)

Major W.G. Barker, a Canadian attached to an RAF squadron, was awarded the Victoria Cross for a heroic single-handed battle against overwhelming odds. Having shot down a German two-seater, he was attacked by at least 15 Fokker DVIIs, the finest German fighter aircraft of the Great War. He was wounded three times but managed to shoot down three of the opponents before crash-landing in Allied territory.

The Sopwith Snipe saw service with the Australian Flying Corps, Brazilian Naval Aviation, the Canadian Air Force and, after the Great War, the Soviet Air Force.

By the end of the war, 264 Snipes had been built. The total number eventually constructed was close to 500. After the war, the Snipe became the standard RAF fighter and some were deployed to Russia to fight on the side of the White Russians during the Russian Civil War. The Canadian Air Force operated the Snipe until 1923. By the time the RAF phased out its Snipes in 1926, it was beginning to look obsolete against the emerging generation of new fighters.

Sopwith TF 2 Salamander

Since 1915, the Western Front had consisted of an unbroken series of trenches running from the Channel coast of Belgium to Switzerland. Even by the shortest route, this was more than 400 miles (640km), but given that both sides in the conflict had frontline trenches and a series of reserve and supply trenches, the complete trench network was several thousand miles in length. It was also largely static and provided soldiers with a level of security and shelter against all but the most direct artillery hit.

Both sides in the conflict developed aircraft specifically to attack the opponent's trench network. This was dangerous work because it required low-level flying, often in a straight line, making the aircraft and pilots vulnerable to fire from machine guns and even small arms from the ground. Germany had tackled this challenge with, among others, the Junkers J.1, which was an all-metal aeroplane except for some fabric covering on the rear fuselage. Steel plate protected the vulnerable areas.

Although somewhat late in the day, the Sopwith Salamander was designed as a single-seat scout armoured for trench fighting and ground-attack missions. Until its arrival on the Western Front these tasks had been undertaken in aircraft that were unsuitable for high-level fighting, but were more effective at lower altitudes.

During the Third Battle of Ypres, better known as Passchendaele, which was fought from July to November 1917, the Airco DH.5 was the prime aircraft in use and actually proved effective, but casualties were high. Due to the heavy losses, the RFC asked Sopwith to modify a Sopwith Camel for this role with downward firing guns and protective armour. A modified Camel was duly produced and designated TF.1, the TF standing for 'Trench Fighter'. A pair of Lewis machine guns was fitted to fire downwards at an angle of 45 degrees. Because it proved impossible for the pilot to aim the guns, the TF.1 did not go into production but was used for testing.

In early 1918, work began in earnest on what was viewed as an armoured version of the Sopwith Snipe.

The Salamander was based on the Sopwith Snipe albeit with a slab-sided fuselage, a 12in (30cm) greater wingspan and a slightly shorter fuselage, but there were steel plates fitted beneath the belly of the aircraft, and around the cockpit and the fuel tanks. In effect, the forward part of the fuselage was an armour plate box, which weighed 605lb (275kg) protecting the pilot and fuel supply. The rear of

The Sopwith Salamander ground-attack aircraft. (Picryl)

the fuselage was a conventional wood and fabric structure, but flat sided. The wings and tailplane were identical in structure to the Snipe except that they had been strengthened to cope with the extra weight. The wingspan was 31ft 2in (9.42m) and the length was 18ft 9in (5.72m).

Unfortunately, only three Salamanders had reached France by October 1918 and another two were in existence, these being issued to training units.

The aircraft was well equipped for its role. Initially the plan was to have a fixed Vickers machine gun firing through the propeller arc with Constantinesco gear and two Lewis guns mounted to fire through the cockpit floor at an angle of 45 degrees, as with the Camel T.F.1. This was changed to twin synchronised Vickers machine guns before the prototype's first flight. Four 25lb (10kg) bombs could be carried.

The 200hp (149kW) Bentley rotary motor gave a top speed of 123.5mph (198km/h) and a service ceiling of 13,000ft (3,960m), although given its role, the ceiling was academic. The aircraft carried 29 imperial gallons (130 litres/35 US gallons) of fuel.

The first prototype had its maiden flight in April 1918 and was sent to France for service evaluation on 9 May. On 19 May, it was wrecked when the pilot crashed while avoiding a tender crossing the aerodrome. Although, the results were broadly favourable for the role envisaged, lateral control was seen as poor. The tail and ailerons were modified to resolve the problem.

An initial order for 500 Salamanders was placed in June 1918, and additional orders were placed with a variety of sub-contractors, bringing the total number to 1,400. However, delivery problems with the steel plates and the Bentley B.R.2 engines delayed production and by the time the first fully equipped Salamander squadron was due to fly to France, the war was over.

Production continued for some time after the Armistice, and more than 200 were eventually built although 70 were fitted with Snipe wings, rather than those intended for the Salamander, rendering the aircraft unsafe. In practice, the armoured steel plates caused some distortion of the airframe, making the aircraft dangerous. Although some Salamanders were used for experimentation with disorientation colour schemes in 1919, and some were in use in Egypt in 1922, the Salamander had a short life.

With the benefit of hindsight, failure to continue the development of specialist ground-attack aircraft was an opportunity lost.

Fairey III

The prototype of the Fairey III family of seaplanes was designed and built by the Fairey Aviation Company of Hayes, Middlesex, and Hamble on Southampton Water, in response to an Admiralty Specification, N.2(a), for a carrier-based seaplane for the RNAS. It had folding wings and was powered by a 260hp (194kW) Sunbeam Maori engine. It was tested with both the floatplanes and with a wheeled undercarriage.

Orders were placed for Fairey IIIs with both arrangements. The wheeled version was known as the IIIA, and the floatplanes IIIB. Fifty of the IIIAs were built, but only 28 of the IIIBs were constructed before an improved version, the IIIC, became available, fitted with the 375hp (280kW) Rolls-Royce Eagle VIII motor.

The Fairey IIIC was a two-seat bomber and reconnaissance seaplane and 38 were built. It had a top speed of 110mph (184km/h) and a service ceiling of up to 15,500ft (4,725m) depending on the load. Its high performance meant that it could function as a two-seat fighter aircraft, if necessary. During the Great War, it was employed on escort duties over the North Sea and the British and French coasts.

A squadron of Fairy IIICs was used in the North Russian Expeditionary Force of 1919. The Fairey IIIC was used for many years after the war. A significant achievement was the first East-West crossing (in stages) of the South Atlantic in 1922.

The wingspan was 36ft 9in (11.2m) and the length was 46ft 2in (14.05m).

Development of the Fairey III family of aircraft continued after the end of the Great War, the last version entering service in 1927. These versions are described in the book *British Military Biplanes: 1920–40*.

The Fairey IIIC. (Roger Staker)

Vickers Vimy

The Vickers Vimy was designed and manufactured by Vickers Ltd during 1917, as a heavy bomber for the RFC. The interest in heavy bombers followed the German Gotha raids on London. At the end of July, the Air Board placed an order for Handley Page O/100 bombers and also orders for prototype heavy bombers from Handley Page and Vickers. This was followed in mid-August by a contract for three prototypes.

Vickers started work on the design of a large twin-engine bomber intended to be powered by either Royal Aircraft Factory 4D motors or 200hp (149kW) Hispano-Suiza motors. Vickers' chief designer, Reginald 'Rex' Pierson, discussed the proposal with the Air Board to reach an accord on a proposed night bomber that could attack targets within the German Empire. It would be called the Vimy after the Battle of Vimy Ridge in April 1917.

The design and construction were conventional, but the fuselage was made of steel tubing, and was fabric covered. The wingspan was 68ft 1in (20.75m) and its length 43ft 7in (13.28m).

The Vimy was designed to carry a crew of three and 12 250lb (113kg) bombs. The pilot was positioned just ahead of the wings and there was a nose gunner, with another gunner behind the wings, each with a pair of Scarff-mounted Lewis machine guns. Most of the bombs were carried internally, set vertically between the spars of the lower centre section. The Vimy could also carry two torpedoes.

The first prototype Vimy was flown on 30 November 1917. This aircraft was fitted with 207hp (154kW) Hispano Suiza motors, the second prototype was powered by 260hp (194kW) Sunbeam Maoris, the third by 300hp (224kW) Fiat A-12s, and the fourth by 360hp (268kW) Rolls-Royce Eagle VIIIs, which became

The Vickers Vimy, named after the famous battle of Vimy Ridge. (Picryl)

the standard. With these motors, the Vimy had a maximum speed of 103mph (165km/h), a service ceiling of 7,000ft (2,134m) and a maximum range of 900 miles (1,440km).

During testing, each of the first three prototypes suffered problems. The engines of the first aircraft proved unreliable and it was returned for modification. Even so, on 26 March 1918, an order for 150 aircraft was placed. The engines of the second had unreliable cooling systems, and it was written off when it crashed following engine failure. The third was lost on 11 September when the bombs it was carrying exploded following a hard landing due to a pilot-induced stall.

Production was already under way and the configuration of the fourth prototype set the standard, although a variety of engines were installed as supply and demand challenges emerged. The first order was met by Vickers, although only 13 had been completed by the end of 1918. In May 1918, additional orders had been placed with sub-contractors including Westland Aircraft, Clayton & Shuttleworth and the Royal Aeronautical Establishment. After the war, a number of contract cancellations took place, and the total number of Vimys actually built is believed to be about 230.

The Vimy arrived on the Western Front too late to be used operationally. However, it continued to be a frontline bomber in the UK and the Middle East until 1925. It equipped a Special Reserve bomber squadron based in Northern Ireland until 1929 and was employed in training and other minor roles until 1938.

The Vimy also served with the Spanish Air Force and commercial versions of the Vimy served with the government of China, and a French airline, Grands Express Aériens. In the UK, Imperial Airways and Instone Air Line were users of the commercial version. Five aircraft were converted as Vimy ambulance aircraft for the RAF. These incorporated a nose-loading door and could accommodate four stretcher cases or eight sitting patients plus two medical attendants.

No history of the Vimy would be complete without reference to the first non-stop transatlantic flight on 14/15 June 1919. The story began when the *Daily Mail* newspaper offered a prize of £10,000 to the 'the aviator who shall first cross the Atlantic in an aeroplane in flight from any point in the United States of America, Canada or Newfoundland to any point in Great Britain or Ireland in 72 continuous hours'.

Several teams entered the competition, which actually started from St John's, Newfoundland. The Vimy, with pilot John Alcock and navigator Arthur Brown, took off at 1.45pm local time. The flight was beyond challenging, with bitter cold and a snowstorm to contend with, which could easily have brought the aircraft down. Even so, at 8.40am they landed near Clifden, County Galway, Ireland. The aircraft suffered some damage on landing because what had looked like a field from the air proved to be Derrigimlagh Bog!

The final derivative of the Vickers Vimy was the Vickers Vernon. This aircraft is described in *British Military Biplanes: 1920–40*.

Felixstowe F.3 Canada

The Felixstowe F.3 was a larger version of the Felixstowe F.2A. The prototype first flew in February 1917 powered by two 320hp (239kW) Sunbeam Cossack engines. Its larger size gave it a greater range and more bombload, but it was not as fast or manoeuvrable as the F.2A.

Even so, substantial orders followed with production aircraft being powered by two 345hp (257kW) Rolls-Royce Eagle VIII engines. These gave a maximum speed of 91mph (147km/h), a service ceiling of 8,000ft (2,438m) and an endurance of six hours.

The F.3 had a crew of four, and was not popular with its crews. The aircraft served with the RNAS primarily in the Mediterranean; in fact, the need for aircraft of this type was so urgent that 18 were constructed in Malta. Although the eventual number of orders was in the region of 260, only about 100 were completed by the end of the war.

In the 1920s, the F.3 was used to establish the feasibility of some long-distance routes, including the first trans-Canada flight in 1920 and the first flight between mainland Portugal and Madeira in 1921.

The wingspan was 102ft (31.09m) and the length was 49ft 2in (14.99m). Armament was a Lewis machine gun in the nose and three Lewis machine guns amidships. Up to 920lb (420kg) of bombs could be carried under the wings.

In addition to the RAF and RNAS, users of the Felixstowe F.3 were Australia (commercial use), Canadian Air Board, Portuguese Naval Aviation, Aeronautica Naval Espana and the United States Navy.

The Felixstowe F.3 had a long-range capability. (Picryl)

Parnall Panther

In 1917, the Admiralty issued Specification N.2A for a two-seat reconnaissance and spotting aircraft capable of operating from aircraft carriers. The Parnall Aircraft Company was a Bristol-based company and had recruited Harold Bolas who had been deputy designer at the Admiralty Air Department. With his knowledge and skills, the company planned to meet the specification's requirements.

The Panther's wings were conventional wood and fabric, but it was fitted with a birch plywood monocoque fuselage capable of being folded for storage. The fuselage was hinged behind the observer's cockpit. Flotation bags were fitted. The wingspan was 29ft 6in (8.99m) and the length was 24ft 11in (7.99m).

The prototype Panther, at this time called the Parnall N.2A, flew in 1917 and was evaluated at the A&AEE in May 1918. These tests proved to be a disappointment. Both the top speed and climb rate were only slightly better than existing RNAS aircraft. However, it was decided to continue with the Parnall aircraft and it was returned for flotation gear to be fitted.

Parnall produced a further five N.2A prototypes. The second of these was sent for Fleet trials on 22 June 1918 and was taken aboard the battle-cruiser HMS *Repulse*. The third aircraft was completed in July 1918 and flew to the Isle of Grain Naval Experimental Station for ditching trials. For these, Parnall's flotation gear had been replaced by the Isle of Grain standard equipment.

The fourth and fifth aircraft were sent for trials at the Royal Aircraft Establishment and Fleet trials respectively. Finally, the sixth machine was officially called the Parnall Panther and regarded as the production standard aircraft.

An order for 300 of the type was placed in 1918. However, when the war ended, this order was reduced to 150. In the meantime, Parnall Aircraft Company had been sold to W. & T. Avery Ltd and this company would not accept the reduction. As a result, the order was transferred to Bristol Aeroplane Company which completed construction of the Panthers between 1919 and 1920.

It was powered by a 230hp (170kW) Bentley BR.2 air-cooled 9-cylinder rotary engine.

The Panther served with reconnaissance units on board two carriers, but although the aircraft handled well, the Bentley engines proved unreliable and the system of arrester wires in place at that time was unsatisfactory, which resulted in a number of accidents.

The Panther remained in service with the Fleet Air Arm until 1926. In 1920, two were sold to the US Navy and during 1921–22 another 12 were sold to the Imperial Japanese Navy.

A Parnall Panther. (Picryl)

Nieuport Nighthawk

The Nieuport and General Aircraft Company Ltd was established in November 1916 by Samuel Waring owner of the furniture company Waring & Gillow. Its objective was to build French Nieuport fighters under licence. The company constructed 50 Nieuport 17 *bis* aircraft before changing to build Sopwith Camels and, after the war, Sopwith Snipes. The company delivered 400 Camels and 100 Snipes before closing in 1920.

Aircraft design and construction by the Royal Aircraft Factory at Farnborough came to an end in 1917 following an official inquiry known as the Burbidge Report. Nieuport and General seized the opportunity to recruit Henry Folland as Chief Designer from the Royal Aircraft Factory. He had been responsible for the S.E.5A and clearly had a well-deserved reputation as a designer.

Henry Folland designed the Nieuport Nighthawk as a single-seat scout in response to an Air Ministry specification for a fighter to replace the Sopwith Snipe. The proposed aircraft was to be powered by a new engine, the A.B.C. Dragonfly, which was a radial engine under development but expected to deliver 340hp (254kW). The engine was ordered into large-scale production given its promise of high power and low weight. The Nighthawk was built with wood and fabric in a conventional manner. The wingspan was 28ft (8.53m) and the length was 18ft (5.49m).

In August 1918, an order for 150 Nighthawks was placed, long before either aircraft or flight-ready engines were available. The first prototype flew in the late spring of 1919, but proved far from reliable with high fuel consumption and overheating serious enough to cause charring of the propeller hubs. As a result, the order was cancelled.

Nieuport and General, together with a sub-contractor, Gloucestershire Aircraft Company, completed 70 Nighthawks, and another 54 airframes, without engines, were also built. When Nieuport and General closed in August 1920, the rights to the Nighthawk were purchased by Gloster Aircraft Company. Henry Folland also joined that company as chief designer.

The Nighthawk never saw operational service, although a small number went to the Royal Aeronautical Establishment at Farnborough for experimental purposes.

The Nieuport Nighthawk. (PIcryl)

Sopwith Dragon

Air Ministry interest in the 320hp (239kW) ABC Dragonfly I radial engine encouraged the fitting of this engine to the sixth prototype Sopwith Snipe, with an increase in fuselage length of 22in (56cm) to compensate for the additional weight of the Dragonfly.

When the engine worked properly the performance proved encouraging, but there were persistent ignition problems. Even so, convinced by the potential of the engine and the performance, in June 1918, the RAF issued an order for 30 Dragonfly-engined Snipes, an aircraft that became named as the Sopwith Dragon.

Soon the 'new' version of the engine was available, the 360hp (268kW) Dragonfly IA. In late November, the order for the Snipes was cancelled and a new order for 300 Sopwith Dragons was issued in its place.

The prototype Dragon with its new engine began evaluation trials at the A&AEE in February 1919. It achieved a top speed of 150mph (240km/h) and a service ceiling of 25,000ft (620m). However, difficulties with the Dragonfly engine persisted and despite extensive efforts over a long period of time, they were never resolved.

Sopwith continued to build Dragon airframes but only a few aircraft were actually completed with the Dragonfly engines, and none were issued to squadrons. About 200 airframes were built and put into storage awaiting engines that would never arrive. The Dragon was eventually declared obsolete in April 1923.

The Sopwith Dragon was equipped with twin forward-firing Vickers machine guns. Its wingspan was 31ft 1in (9.47m) and its length was 21ft 9in (6.63m).

The Sopwith Dragon displays its unfortunate engine. (Picryl)

Experimental and Prototype Aircraft

Royal Aircraft Factory B.E.4

It was in December 1911 when the Royal Aircraft Factory began design work on an aircraft with a similar layout to the B.E.2, but with a rotary engine rather than the air-cooled in-line engine, which powered the B.E.2. The fuselage was mounted between the wings, and was set clear of both the lower and upper wings. There were no ailerons, lateral control being achieved by wing warping.

Two aircraft were built in early 1912, designated B.E.3 and B.E.4. The first to fly (B.E.3) was powered by a 50hp (37kW) Gnome Omega rotary engine. Geoffrey de Havilland piloted the aircraft on its maiden flight on 3 May 1912 and had sufficient confidence in it that he took passengers up on the same day. On 13 May, it was delivered to the RFC.

The second aircraft (B.E.4) was also initially powered by the Gnome Omega engine when it first flew on 24 June 1912. It was passed to the RFC in August, and was re-engined in September with a 70hp (52kW) Gnome engine. At least two more Gnome Omega-equipped aircraft were constructed by private contractors in late 1912–early 1913.

The B.E.3 and B.E.4 aircraft were attached to No.3 Squadron and were used for a variety of trials. B.E.4 crashed, possibly due to metal fatigue, which made the rudder fail, on 11 March 1914, on Salisbury Plain, killing the crew of two. With appropriate modifications the remaining aircraft continued until the summer of 1914.

The Royal Aircraft Factory B.E.4. (Picryl)

Avro 501 and 503

The Avro 501 was designed as a two-seat seaplane, although the objective was for it to be amphibious. In early 1913, the prototype was tested on Lake Windermere, powered by a 100hp (75kW) Gnome engine. It was then converted from a single float with outriggers to a twin-float configuration and it was purchased by the Admiralty. The twin-float arrangement proved to be too heavy for the engine and it was apparently converted again, this time to a landplane.

Improvements were made and the next machine was designated the Avro 503. On 28 May 1913, the first flight took off from the River Adur at Shoreham, where Avro had its base. The passenger on board, John Alcock, would later become part of the celebrated duo who carried out the first air crossing of the Atlantic Ocean.

Three Avro 503s were ordered for naval use and delivered. In June 1913, the prototype 503 was demonstrated to a senior officer from the Imperial German Navy and it was purchased by the German government. In September, it flew from Wilhelmshaven to Heligoland, across part of the North Sea, a distance of 40 miles (64km). The German company Gotha purchased a licence from Avro to build its own version of the 503, called the WD.1.

Other German companies built unlicenced versions, including Albatros, Friedrichshafen and AGO. Some WD.1s were provided to the Ottoman Empire when the German Navy finished with them.

The 503 had a 100hp (75kW) Gnome Omega rotary engine giving a top speed of 55mph (88km/h). The upper wingspan was 50ft 6in (15.39m) and the length was 33ft 6in (10.21m). There was a single Avro 501 built, and four Avro 503 aircraft.

Avro 503 floatplane. (Picryl)

Royal Aircraft Factory F.E.3

In 1913, the Royal Aircraft Factory designed a remarkably unusual aircraft, which was designated the F.E.3 and also known as the A.E.1 (Armed Experimental). It was intended that the F.E.3 would carry a shell-firing weapon produced by the Coventry Ordnance Works. Each shell weighed 1.5lb (0.68kg) and although the gun was 'quick-loading' it seems unlikely that the F.E.3 would have been able to carry a large number of these shells.

An unusual feature of the F.E.3s design was that the tail assembly was carried on a single boom, which was connected to the propeller via bearings, rather than the twin-boom layout normally applied to pusher aircraft. The gunner and the pilot sat in tandem fashion in a wood and metal nacelle. The 100hp (75kW) water-cooled in-line engine was fitted in the nose of the aircraft and drove a four-blade propeller via a shaft running under the cockpit, with a chain drive providing the final linkage to the propeller itself.

The gun was mounted in the aircraft nose and was intended to fire through the engine's air intake.

The F.E.3 had its first flight in the summer of 1913, but during one flight the propeller broke resulting in a forced landing. It had become apparent that the tail boom was not strong enough to achieve safe flight and no attempt was made to resume flight testing. However, the gun installation was test fired in a static situation and the recoil was not considered excessive.

The F.E.3 had a maximum speed of 75mph (121km/h) and a service ceiling of 5,000ft (1,500m). Its wingspan was 40ft (12.19m) and its length was 29ft 3in (8.92m).

The unusual Royal Aircraft Factory F.E.3. (Picryl)

Royal Aircraft Factory S.E.2

In 1912, Geoffrey de Havilland, designer with the Royal Aircraft Factory, began work on a single-seat scout or unarmed fast reconnaissance aircraft. It is perhaps the first aircraft in the world designed from scratch for such a role. It was a tractor aircraft called the B.S.1, for Bleriot Scout in recognition of Bleriot's pioneering of the tractor configuration.

The fuselage was a wooden monocoque construction of circular section to the rear of the cockpit. There were no ailerons, lateral control being achieved by wing warping. Initially there was a small rudder but no fixed fin. The engine installed was a Gnome rotary engine rated at 100hp (75kW), although in practice it only delivered about 82hp (61kW).

Early in 1913, Geoffrey de Havilland flew the B.S.1 for its maiden flight. Its performance was remarkably good, achieving nearly 92mph (148km/h) and a rate of climb of 900ft per minute (4.6m/sec). Not surprisingly the small rudder did not satisfy de Havilland and he designed a replacement. Before this could be fitted, he crashed the B.S.1 on 27 March 1913, badly damaging the aircraft and suffering a broken jaw.

The machine was rebuilt with modified tail surfaces incorporating a conventional fin, a larger rudder, proper elevators and an 80hp (60kW) Gnome engine. Although briefly described as the B.S.2, the aircraft was quickly designated as the S.E.2 (Scout Experimental), a type of designation that applied to virtually all Royal Aircraft Factory products.

The S.E.2 had its first flight in October 1913, but was rebuilt in April 1914. This time, it was supervised by Henry Folland following Geoffrey de Havilland's move to the Aircraft Manufacturing Company (Airco) as chief designer. The changes to the S.E.2 were mainly to the tail surfaces with a new tailplane and elevators, together with a larger fin and larger rudder. The monocoque fuselage was replaced with conventional wood and fabric covering, being cheaper to mass produce, and attention was given to the streamlining of struts and bracing wires. This revised aircraft first flew on 3 October 1914.

On 27 October, it was despatched to France to join an operational squadron. Given that France was now a war zone, the S.E.2 was equipped with a pair of rifles fitted to the sides of the fuselage and angled outwards to avoid hitting the propeller. The pilot was also given a revolver. It remained with No. 3 Squadron until March 1915 when it was damaged by a bomb explosion and returned to England. It had been strongly praised for its speed and manoeuvrability.

The S.E.2 had a wingspan of 27ft 6¼in (8.39m) and a length of 20ft 10in (6.35m). It had pointed the way for one of the most successful British fighters of the Great War, the S.E.5A.

The Royal Aircraft Factory S.E.2. (Picryl)

Royal Aircraft Factory H.R.E.2

The H.R.E.2 was designed as a reconnaissance floatplane for the Royal Navy. The letters stood for Hydroplane Reconnaissance Experimental. The word 'hydroplane' indicated that the proposed aircraft would be a seaplane or floatplane. When the H.R.E.2 was designed, it was in response to a specification supplied by the Air Department of the Admiralty for the Naval Wing of the Royal Flying Corps, the RNAS having yet to be established.

The resulting aircraft was a two-seat floatplane with flat sides to the fuselage and a rounded decking. The pilot was positioned in the rear cockpit just behind the trailing edge of the upper wing. There were no ailerons, lateral control being achieved by wing warping.

Although designed from scratch as a floatplane, the first flight in 1913 took place with a landplane configuration and was powered by a 70hp (52kW) Renault air-cooled in-line engine. Having been tested as a landplane, the aircraft was modified by upgrading the engine to a 100hp (75kW) Renault engine and floats were fitted. These were conventional for the time, a pair of short floats mounted under the lower wing and supported by struts attached to the fuselage, together with a small double float under the tail assembly. The rudder was also modified with a large teardrop-shaped rudder positioned clear of the elevator hinge and enabling full movement of the elevators.

While attempting to take off from Frensham Pond in Surrey, the aircraft was seriously damaged. As a result, it was rebuilt as a landplane, but ailerons were fitted and the undercarriage had skids that projected forwards to help prevent a nose-over. In this form, the H.R.E.2 served with the RNAS until the beginning of the Great War. It was eventually wrecked in a crash on 10 February 1915.

The aircraft had a top speed of 60mph (97km/h). Its wingspan was 32ft 3in (9.83m) and its length was 45ft 3.5in (13.8m).

The Royal Aircraft Factory H.R.E.2. (Picryl)

Royal Aircraft Factory B.E.9

The B.E.9 was an endeavour by the Royal Aircraft Factory to marry the performance benefits of a tractor aircraft with the ability to provide an accurate field of fire for the observer/gunner, which a 'pusher' configuration offered. This was before the 'breakthrough' of synchronisation of gun and propeller changed the shape of aerial combat forever.

The approach taken was to modify a B.E.2c. This involved removing the observer's cockpit from behind the pilot, moving the engine back and constructing a wooden nacelle or 'pulpit' in front of the engine in which the hapless observer/gunner now sat with a Lewis machine gun.

Although this seemed to have solved the twin problems of tractor versus pusher performance and ability to deliver fire power where required, the arrangement created its own challenges. The most serious in an operational sense was that virtually all communication between the observer and pilot was lost given that the engine was now between them. Then there was the safety of the observer in the 'pulpit'. He was immediately in front of the propeller and any sudden or unexpected movement could prove fatal. In the event of a crash or even a nose-over on landing, the unfortunate observer would be crushed by the engine.

The prototype first flew on 14 August 1915. There was little noticeable difference in performance from the basic B.E.2c on which the B.E.9 was based. In September, it was sent to France for service trials. During this time, a small number of operational patrols were undertaken including one in which it is understood an encounter with a Fokker Eindekker occurred. The feedback from the RFC was negative, with the B.E.9 being labelled as dangerous to the observer. In early 1916, the machine was returned to Britain and no further action was taken.

The B.E.9 was powered by a Royal Aircraft Factory R.A.F.1a engine of 90hp (67kW) giving a top speed of 82mph (132km/h). The wingspan was larger than the B.E.2c at 40ft 10½in (12.46m) and its length was 29ft (8.84m).

The Royal Aircraft Factory B.E.9 showing its suicidal observer's pulpit. (Picryl)

Sopwith Bee

The Sopwith Bee was a one-off diminutive aircraft designed by Sopwith's chief designer, Harry Hawker. It became his personal runabout, powered by a 50hp (37kW) Gnome Omega rotary engine. There were no ailerons, lateral control being exercised by wing warping. Given the small dimensions of the Bee, positioning the pilot close to the centre of gravity posed a challenge, which seems to have been met by creating a semi-circular aperture in the trailing edge of the upper wing to accommodate the pilot's head, thus enabling him or her to sit at the centre of gravity.

It is believed that the Sopwith Bee had its first flight in late 1915 or 1916. The importance of the Sopwith Bee is the influence it had on subsequent Sopwith designs. The most immediate of these was the Sopwith Pup, which in some ways was a direct descendant of the Bee.

The Bee had a wingspan of only 16ft 3in (4.95m) and a length of 14ft 3in (4.34m).

The Sopwith Bee, Harry Hawker's runabout. (via Key Archives)

Airco DH3

The Aircraft Manufacturing Company developed the DH3 as a private venture. It was designed by Geoffrey de Havilland as a long-range day bomber. For its time, it was a large aircraft with a wingspan of 60ft 10in (18.54m) and a length of 36ft 10in (11.23m).

Power was provided by two 120hp (89kW) Beardmore six-cylinder, in-line water-cooled engines mounted between the wings in pusher configuration. It had its first flight very early in 1916. It proved to have a top speed of 95mph (153km/h), a range of 700 miles (1,100km) and an endurance of eight hours, but its rate of climb was not considered adequate.

A second prototype was built with more powerful Beardmore engines of 160hp (120kW). This attracted a production order for 50 aircraft from the War Office. However, the order was cancelled before an aircraft could be built. One reason was the rate of climb, which at nearly an hour to reach 6,500ft (1,981m) was viewed as poor, but it is also possible that the Air Ministry officials viewed strategic bombing as simply not worthwhile. If so, this is a pity, because the DH3 was one of the first aircraft capable of making long-range bombing a practical proposition to targets as far away as Berlin.

In 1917, both prototypes were scrapped, but lessons learned were applied in the design of the DH.10 Amiens.

The Airco DH3. (via Key Archives)

Vickers F.B.12

The story of the Vickers F.B.12 began early after the outbreak of the Great War, when Vickers and a company called Hart Engine Company formed a partnership to develop a nine-cylinder radial engine. The intention was that this engine would power a range of new aircraft designs produced by Vickers. The first demonstration of this alliance was to be a single-seat pusher fighter called the Vickers F.B.12. Although the raised nacelle greatly improved visibility compared with the de Havilland DH.2 and the Royal Aircraft Factory FE.8, it shared their configuration, which was becoming obsolete.

The wings were constructed from wood and were fabric covered. The nacelle was of circular cross-section. It had a steel tube framework, was fabric covered, and the twin tail booms were steel and came together to support the tail structure. The F.B.12 was equipped with a single Lewis machine gun fitted inside the nacelle with only the barrel protruding.

The first example flew in June 1916, but because the Hart engine was not yet available it was powered by an 80hp (60kW) Le Rhone rotary engine. With this engine it was underpowered and a 100hp (75kW) Gnome Monosoupape engine was fitted in its place. It was then rebuilt with increased wingspan and wing area and in December 1916, it was sent to France for testing in an operational environment. Initial feedback was encouraging, indicating that it was as good as the DH.2 and the F.E.8. Unfortunately, both were heavily outclassed by the new German Albatros D.1.

The first aircraft (designated F.B.12B) to be fitted with the Hart engine had its maiden flight in early 1917, but in the meantime, the War Office had placed an order for 50 aircraft for the RFC, all to be powered by the Hart engine. Sadly the F.B.12B crashed during tests early in 1917, with the result that Vickers abandoned the Hart relationship.

Only 18 of the order were built and they were fitted with a variety of engines. None saw operational service on the Western Front, although one was delivered to a Home Defence unit.

With the 100hp (75kW) Gnome Monosoupape engine, the F.B.12 had a top speed of 86mph (138km/h) and a service ceiling of 11,500ft (3,500m). Its upper wingspan was 26ft (7.92m) and its length 21ft 6in (6.55m).

Vickers F.B.12 fighter. (Picryl)

Bristol Scout F

1916 was a difficult year for the RFC and RNAS as new German aircraft such as the Albatros D.I appeared in the skies over the Western Front. Air superiority required British and Allied fighter aircraft with sufficient performance and capability to deliver a competitive advantage in the air. Unfortunately, towards the end of 1916, engines of sufficient power were in very short supply. One engine that could potentially achieve this was the Hispano Suiza 8. However, it was unreliable and supplies were in any case targeted at the Royal Aircraft Factory S.E.5a.

In an endeavour to break this circle, the British and Colonial Aircraft Company's designer, Frank Barnwell, designed a single-seat Scout based on a proposed 200hp (150kW) 10-cylinder water-cooled radial engine, to be called the Bristol Scout E. When this engine failed to materialise, the search for a suitable replacement continued. The company managed to secure an order from the Air Ministry for six aircraft together with a promise of some 200hp (150kW) Hispano Suiza V8 engines.

By June 1917, these had been replaced by 200hp (150mkW) Sunbeam Arab water-cooled radials. With these engines, the aircraft was redesignated as the Bristol Scout F. The upper wings carried ailerons and there were cut-outs in the centre section to improve the pilot's view. The coolant header tank was situated in a small bulge on top of the cowling and the radiator was positioned between the undercarriage legs, with two shutters to enable control of coolant temperature.

The Sunbeam Arab engine suffered from vibrations and Bristol decided to fit it only to the first two aircraft. The first of these flew in March 1918. It was very fast, with a speed of 138mph (221km/h) and could climb to 10,000ft (3,050m) in 9 minutes 30 seconds. The second aircraft was evaluated at the Central Flying School by an experienced pilot who judged it a better aerobatic aircraft than the S.E.5a.

Bristol was approached by a local (to Bristol) firm called Cosmos Engineering. It was looking for an airframe to test its 315hp (235kW) Cosmos Mercury radial engine, which was under development. As a result, the third Bristol Scout F was fitted with this engine. It reduced the length of the aircraft by 10in (25cm), but the weight increased by 60lb (27kg). It first flew on 6 September 1918. The top speed, compared with the Sunbeam Arab machine, increased only slightly, probably because the added weight counter-balanced the increased power. By contrast the rate of climb was much better.

The Bristol Scout F was armed with two Vickers machine guns. The Mercury engine gave it a top speed of 145mph (233km/h). The upper wingspan was 29ft 7in (9.02m) and the length was 20ft (6.1m).

The fourth airframe was built, but only as a spare. The Armistice brought to an end the Cosmos Mercury contract, the cancellation of the contracts for the remaining Bristol Scout Fs and all hopes of production of what might have been a very successful Scout.

The life of the Bristol Scout F was curtailed by the Armistice. (Picryl)

Royal Aircraft Factory F.E.9

In the summer of 1916, the Royal Aircraft Factory embarked on the design of a two-seat fighter as a replacement for the F.E.2. Despite the fact that reliable synchronisation gearing was now available to enable a tractor fighter to fire through the propeller arc, the company decided to stick with the pusher layout.

The aircraft that emerged was an unusual design. The nacelle was mounted high up to the top of the wing gap and extended far forward of the wings. This gave the observer/gunner an excellent field of view, seated in the nose of the aircraft ahead of the pilot. Dual controls were fitted.

Power was provided by a 200hp Hispano-Suiza 8 water-cooled engine. Top speed was 105mph (168km/h) and the service ceiling was 15,500ft (4,720m). A Lewis machine gun on a Scarff ring was in the observer's cockpit and there was another Lewis gun on a pillar mounting between the two cockpits.

An order for three prototypes and 24 production aircraft was placed. When the first prototype flew in April 1917 it proved a disappointment, with poor climb performance and a serious handling problem caused by over-balanced ailerons, which caused the aircraft to roll on to its back in steep turns. Various changes of rudder and aileron were tried to correct this.

The first prototype was sent to France for trials. Major General Trenchard recommended termination of the development, but a second prototype followed in October 1917 and was used for Home Defence purposes. The third and last aircraft appeared in November 1917 and was used at Farnborough for tests and trials. No further production took place.

The Royal Aircraft Factory F.E.9. (Roger Staker)

Fairey F.2

The Fairey F.2 was designed as a three-seat long-range fighter and was the first aircraft that was entirely designed by the Fairey Aviation Company. It was developed at the request of the Admiralty and the wings folded at the rear of the twin 190hp (142kW) Rolls-Royce Falcon engines. Design began in 1916 and the F.2 had its first flight on 17 May 1917.

By any standards, it was a large aircraft, and as a fighter it was massive with a wingspan of 77ft (23.47m) and a length of 40ft 6in (12.34m). It was armed with two Lewis machine guns, one in the nose and one on a Scarff ring in the cockpit just behind the wings. The undercarriage was a four-wheel construction, almost certainly needed to carry the weight of the aircraft, which was 4,880lb (2,213kg).

Perhaps predictably, the Fairey F.2 was found to be slow with a maximum speed of just 93mph (150km/h) and was difficult to handle. In any case, by the time it was built and flown, the Admiralty had lost interest in the project and there was no further development.

The very large Fairey F.2 long-range fighter. (Picryl)

Kennedy Giant

The Kennedy Giant bomber was the brainchild of Chessborough J. H. Mackenzie-Kennedy who, as an 18-year-old, had left England and travelled to Russia with just three pounds in his pocket. Having designed Russia's first aeroplane, he formed the Kennedy Aeronautic Company in 1909, and in 1911 he met Igor Sikorski and was involved with the design of the first four-engine Sikorski aircraft.

When the Great War commenced, he returned to England and approached the War Office with a proposal for a larger four-engine bomber. With the encouragement shown and with three colleagues, he embarked on the design of what would become the Kennedy Giant. Construction was undertaken by the Gramophone Company Ltd and Fairey Aviation Company Ltd. Both were based in Hayes, Middlesex, but the scale of the aircraft was such that assembly was carried out in the open at Hendon.

The wingspan was 142ft (43m) and the length was 80ft (24m). It stood at 23ft 6in (7.16m) high. Its empty weight was 18,000lb (8,618kg). The four engines were mounted in tractor-pusher fashion in nacelles on the lower wings. Each of the Salmson water-cooled radial engines generated 200hp (150kW).

The fuselage was rectangular in section from nose to tail and all three crew members were contained in fully enclosed cabins.

In late 1917, the Giant was ready for its first flight. The engines were run at full throttle and the ground helped by sloping gently away in the direction of travel. Unfortunately, the well-named Giant managed only a short hop and even then, the tailskid was dragging on the ground. There were no more attempts to fly the Giant and it ended its days derelict at Northolt Aerodrome.

The Kennedy Giant. (Alamy)

Royal Aircraft Factory N.E.1

The Royal Aircraft Factory N.E.1 was a night fighter developed from the Royal Aircraft Factory F.E.9 fighter. Design work started in 1917, and at this stage, the proposed aircraft was designated as the F.E.12. The wing centre sections, tail booms and undercarriage were combined with new outer wings and the tailplane was enlarged. To enable it to be an effective night fighter, it was to be equipped with two searchlights and would be armed with a shell-firing cannon.

The design was then revised with new wings and tail booms, together with a wider undercarriage. This was to be the N.E.1 (Night-flying Experimental).

The pilot and gunner sat in tandem, but with the pilot in front to provide him with the best view. To assist the crew, there was a searchlight fitted in the nose of the aircraft. The gunner was to be armed with either a 1.59in (40mm) breech-loading Vickers QF Gun Mk.II, or a 37mm Coventry Ordnance Works automatic cannon. Both of these were significant weapons akin to light artillery.

The N.E.1 was powered by a 200hp (149kW) Hispano-Suiza 8 water-cooled engine mounted in pusher configuration. There were ailerons on both the upper and lower wings.

On 8 September 1917, the first prototype took to the air for the first time, but crashed on 14 September. It was rebuilt but the searchlight was removed and the gunner, armed with the Vickers QF Gun, was moved in front of the pilot. An externally mounted, fixed, Lewis machine gun was fitted on the starboard side of the fuselage for the pilot to operate. Now modified, the N.E.1 flew on 4 October 1917.

In tests, it proved easy to fly and the gunner now had an excellent field of view, however, a test report suggested that it was doubtful if the performance was good enough for suitability as a night fighter. Six prototypes were completed, the second of these being sent to No.78 Squadron, and the others being used for various trials.

The N.E.1 had a top speed of 95mph (153km/h) and a service ceiling of 17,500ft (5,300m), with an endurance of two hours 45 minutes. The wingspan was 47ft 10in (14.58m) and the length was 28ft 6in (8.69m).

Royal Aircraft Factory N.E.1 night fighter. (Picryl)

Sopwith Hippo

The Sopwith Hippo was another aircraft designed with a view to replacing one coming towards the end of its operational service, given the need to strive for aerial advantage. The target for the Hippo was the Sopwith 1½ Strutter in use by the Armee de l'Air.

The Hippo was designed in summer 1917 and although the Air Ministry did not place an order, it granted Sopwith a licence to build prototypes, but as a private venture. It was a key feature of the Hippo that the aircraft should provide the best possible view for the pilot and gunner. This concept dictated the shape of the aircraft, in particular, the heavy negative stagger of the wings. The upper wing was set back by 2ft 3in (0.69m) with the pilot placed ahead of the wing and the observer/gunner sitting behind the rear spar of the upper wing. The crew's heads were level with the upper wing, with cut-outs in the forward and trailing edges for pilot and gunner. The fuselage effectively filled the space between the two cockpits.

The pilot had two Vickers machine guns, synchronised for the propeller arc, the observer/gunner having two Lewis machine guns mounted on a rocking pillar. The Hippo was powered by the Clerget II rotary engine of 200hp (150kW) chosen, as with the Bulldog, because of its availability.

The first prototype flew on 13 September 1917. On test, it proved to be sluggish and its performance was not as good as the Bristol Fighter, which was already entering service and against which it would inevitably be compared. This ruled out any possibility that the RFC would be interested in ordering the Hippo. Nevertheless, Sopwith persevered by rebuilding the prototype Hippo with less wing stagger, increased dihedral on the upper wing and a revised tail fin. The gunner's pillar was replaced with a Scarff ring and a single Lewis machine gun. With these modifications, it flew again in April 1918 and a second prototype took to the skies in June of that year. There was no further action.

The Clerget engine gave the Hippo a top speed of 115.5mph (185.9km/h) and a service ceiling of 17,000ft (5,200m). The wingspan was 38ft 9in (11.81m) and the Hippo's length was 24ft 6in (7.47m).

The Sopwith Hippo fighter. (Alamy)

Bristol 13 M.R.1

Although wood was the original construction material for aircraft from the earliest examples, and remained the primary material into the 1920s, some manufacturers had begun to consider metal as an advantageous material. It had a robust quality that helped avoid damage during handling and transport and it did not suffer the deterioration that service in tropical regions often caused to wooden frameworks.

On the other hand, woodworking skills were relatively plentiful in Britain and enabled a host of sub-contractors with little or no knowledge of aviation to build aircraft. Even furniture manufacturers such as Waring and Gillow engaged in aircraft manufacture.

The German aircraft manufacturer Junkers had built true all-metal aircraft since December 1915. Bristol had considered metal construction since 1914 without commitment, but shortage of suitable timber caused by the considerable increase in aircraft production prompted a renewed and serious interest at a company level, and at an official level too.

During 1916, Bristol produced a design for a two-seat metal reconnaissance aircraft with the code M.R.1 (Metal Reconnaissance). A contract for two aircraft was received.

Construction of the fuselage was with duralumin sheet, which was varnished to prevent corrosion. It was made in four sections, the front two when bolted together held the engine and the pilot's cockpit. The rear two sections held the observer's cockpit and the tail unit. The monocoque rear sections were double-skinned, with a smooth outer skin riveted to a corrugated inner skin. Bristol found difficulty in making the aluminium wing spars sufficiently rigid, so outsourced the wings to a Gloucester company, the Steel Wing Company. The first prototype was powered by a 140hp (100kW) Hispano-Suiza engine.

Because the wings were not yet ready, Bristol decided to create wooden framework wings for the early flight trials. The first flight was in mid-1917 and the aircraft was delivered to the Air Ministry in October. The second prototype did not fly until late in 1918, when the metal wings were available. This aircraft had a 180hp (130kW) Wolseley Viper engine.

In April 1919, it was delivered to the Royal Aircraft Establishment but was damaged beyond repair at the end of its delivery flight. The first prototype had metal wings fitted in 1918 and was used for testing purposes.

The M.R.1 had a maximum speed of 110mph (177km/h) and an endurance of five hours. Its wingspan was 42ft 2in (12.85m) and its length was 27ft (8.23m).

The metal Bristol 13 M.R.1 reconnaissance aircraft. (Johan Visschenijk, 1000aircraftphotos.com)

Avro 529

Early in 1916 Avro developed a twin-engine bomber designed to meet RFC guidelines for a heavy bomber, and for the RNAS, which was looking for a short-range bomber. The resulting aircraft was called the Avro Pike. It was too late for either, the RFC having ordered the Handley Page O/100 and the RNAS having ordered the Short Bomber.

However, after trials, the Admiralty ordered two prototypes of a larger aircraft to be based on the Pike for long-range bombing missions. The resulting aircraft was the Avro 529.

It was a large twin engine aircraft conventionally constructed from wood and fabric. In order to facilitate wing folding, the wings had no sweep-back, dihedral or stagger. The rectangular fuselage accommodated a crew of three in separate cockpits. The pilot's cockpit was just forward of the wing leading edge, the front gunner/bomb-aimer was in the nose and the rear gunner was situated midway between the trailing edge and the tail. Interestingly this position was equipped with emergency dual controls. Both gunners had a single Lewis machine gun mounted on a Scarff ring.

The prototypes were fitted with different engines. The first Avro 529 had two 190hp (140kW) Rolls-Royce Falcon water-cooled engines mounted midway between the wings. These drove four-bladed wooden propellers in opposite directions, thus eliminating engine torque. A fuel tank in the centre fuselage held 140 imperial gallons (636 litres/168 US gallons).

The second prototype, designated Avro 529A, was powered by two 230hp (170kW) BHP water-cooled engines mounted in nacelles on the lower wings. These engines drove two-bladed propellers. Fuel was held in separate tanks for each nacelle, each holding 60 imperial gallons (273 litres/72 US gallons). The fuel was pumped by wind-driven pumps to 10 imperial gallon (45 litres/12 US gallons) tanks above each engine, the feed to the engines being by gravity. This aircraft also had slightly different wings and was about 8 per cent lighter. There was also a prone bomb-aimer's position. It could carry 20 50lb (20kg) bombs on racks inside the fuselage.

The Avro 529 and 529A were low powered although otherwise handled reasonably well. There were no production orders and no further development took place.

With the BHP engines the top speed was 116mph (187km/h) and the service ceiling was 17,500ft (5,335m). The wingspan was 64ft 1in (19.53m) and the length was 39ft 8in (12.09m).

The Avro 529 bomber. (Ron D. Myers, 1000aircraftphotos.com)

Short N.2B

British Admiralty Specification N.2B, issued in 1917, called for a long-range patrol seaplane to replace the Short Type 184. Short Brothers response was Short N.2B, a single-engine seaplane with folding wings which Short wanted to fit with a Rolls-Royce Eagle engine.

The Admiralty rejected Short's choice of engine because of an anticipated shortage of the Rolls-Royce Eagle, and a 275hp (205kW) Sunbeam Maori water-cooled engine was substituted. Eight prototype Short N.2Bs were ordered, together with competitor aircraft from Fairey Aviation Company.

The first prototype had its maiden flight in December 1917. In February 1918, it was tested at the Marine Experimental Aircraft Depot on the Isle of Grain. The results were not good. The N.2B had no better performance than the Type 184 with the same engine. Attempts were made to reduce drag and the propeller was changed, but although there was some improvement in performance, the Fairey III was preferred and secured a production contract.

Only the first two Short N.2B aircraft were built. In May 1919, the second prototype was fitted with a Rolls-Royce Eagle engine, which had been salvaged from a modified Short Shirl, which had crashed. With the Eagle engine the Type N.2B had a much improved rate of climb. The top speed was increased by only 8mph (13km/h). As a result, the Sunbeam Maori was re-installed and the aircraft was delivered to the RAF in January 1920.

The Type N.2B was armed with a single Lewis machine gun on a Scarff ring in the rear cockpit. It could carry two 230lb (105kg) bombs under the rear fuselage. Its maximum speed was 92mph (148km/h) with an endurance of four hours 30 minutes and a service ceiling of 10,600ft (3,200m). Its wingspan was 55ft 2in (16.81m) and its length was 40ft 2in (12.24m).

The Short N.2B seaplane. (Johan Visschedijk, 1000aircraftphotos.com)

Fairey N.9

In 1917, Fairey Aviation Company responded to Admiralty Specification N.2(a), which called for a two-seat carrier-based seaplane for the RNAS. Fairey produced two separate designs, one powered by a Rolls-Royce Falcon engine and a second, larger aircraft powered by a Sunbeam Maori motor.

The smaller aircraft, designated the Fairey N.9, had its first flight on 5 July 1917, with the larger aircraft following in September. The N.9 had folding wings and was fitted with trailing edge flaps on both the upper and lower wings. The 200hp (149kW) Rolls-Royce Falcon had radiators fitted on each side of the engine.

On tests the performance of the N.9 was below that required by the specification and no production orders were obtained. It was, however, selected for catapult launching trials. This required some strengthening of the aircraft, and it was then sent to the Marine Experimental Aircraft Depot for the trials to take place. In June 1918, the Fairey N.9 was the first seaplane to be catapult-launched from a Royal Navy ship, HMS *Slinger*.

Fairey purchased the N.9 back from the Royal Navy and fitted it with a Sunbeam Maori engine. In 1920, it was sold to the Royal Norwegian Navy which eventually sold it for civil use in 1927. It was wrecked in a crash in June 1928.

The larger Fairey aircraft proposed against the Admiralty specification was the Fairey III.

With the Rolls-Royce Falcon engine, the N.9 had a maximum speed of 90mph (140km/h) and a service ceiling of 8,600ft (2,600m). The wingspan was 50ft (15.24m) and the N.9 was 35ft 6in (10.82m) long.

The Fairey N.9 carrier-based seaplane. (via Picryl)

Eastchurch Kitten

The Eastchurch Kitten, or more accurately, the Port Victoria P.V.8 Eastchurch Kitten was designed to meet an Admiralty requirement for a small single-seat fighter with a landplane undercarriage, which could fly off short platforms. These platforms were to be fitted to the upper deck of the Royal Navy's destroyers or other small ships, positioned towards the bows. The primary purposes may have been to provide a widely distributed capability to intercept enemy airships.

Orders for a prototype were placed both with the RNAS Experimental Flight at Eastchurch on the Isle of Sheppey, and with the Marine Aircraft Experimental Depot at Port Victoria on the Isle of Grain.

The Eastchurch design was a small aircraft of angular appearance. It was intended to be powered by a 45hp (34kW) ABC Gnat engine and was initially designed to have no fixed tailplane, relying on a balanced elevator. The Kitten was armed with a single Lewis machine gun mounted on the upper wing.

When the prototype Eastchurch Kitten was partly built, the commander of the RNAS Experimental Flight was posted to the Isle of Grain to take command of the Marine Aircraft Experimental Depot. He took with him the part-built Kitten and its designer. The Kitten was given the designation P.V.8 with the competing aircraft being known as the P.V.7.

The Kitten had its first flight on 7 September 1917, but was powered by a 35hp (26kW) ungeared ABC Gnat engine as the planned engine was not available. The Gnat was a two-cylinder horizontally-opposed air-cooled engine. The Kitten was found to be unstable and a small, fixed tailplane and revised elevators were installed. With these modifications, it had better performance and handling than its rival, but the ABC Gnat engine was dreadfully unreliable. Despite praise for the pilot's visibility and handling, the Kitten was viewed as being too fragile for operational use.

No production orders followed, but in March 1918, it was packed up ready for despatch to the US for evaluation. Strangely, there is uncertainty about whether the Kitten was actually sent.

With the 35hp (26kW) ABC Gnat engine, the Kitten had a top speed of 94.5mph (152km/h) and a service ceiling of 14,900ft (4,500m). Its wingspan was just 18ft 11½in (5.78m) and its length 15ft 7½in (4.76m).

The tiny Eastchurch Kitten. (via Picryl)

Westland N.1B

As with design work for almost every new aircraft, the starting point for the Westland N.1B was a specification of requirements, in this case a 1916 Admiralty Specification N.1B. This called for a single-seat flying boat or floatplane fighter to operate from the Royal Navy's seaplane carriers. A top speed of at least 110mph (177km/h) and a service ceiling of 20,000ft (6,100m) were required.

In addition to Westland, Blackburn and Supermarine submitted designs, both for flying boats, whereas Westland proposed a floatplane. An order was placed with Westland for two aircraft. This was the first Westland-designed aircraft. It was a conventional wood and fabric-covered structure. The wings folded for storage and ease of handling on a ship. The trailing edge camber of both the upper and lower wings could be varied to emulate the effect of flaps. Ailerons were fitted to both sets of wings. The engine was an 150hp (110kW) Bentley BR.1 rotary engine.

The first prototype was fitted with twin Sopwith main floats 11ft (3.35m) long and a tail float of 5ft (1.52m). The second prototype had a pair of main floats measuring 17ft 6in (5.34m) in length, obviating the need for a tail float. Armament was a fixed synchronised Vickers machine gun, together with a Lewis machine gun firing over the upper wing.

The first prototype was flown by Harry Hawker in August 1917. Both prototypes were evaluated at the Marine Aircraft Experimental Depot in October 1917. They both demonstrated good handling qualities and performance. Unfortunately for Westland and its N.1B, the RNAS was already operating Sopwith Pups from platforms on board ships, thereby eliminating the need to heave-to in order to lower seaplanes into the water. As a consequence, the N.1B programme was cancelled.

The Westland N.1B had a top speed of 107mph (172km/h) and a service ceiling of 10,400ft (3,200m). The wingspan was 31ft 3½in (9.54m) and the length of the N.1B was 26ft 5½in (8.06m).

The Westland N.1B was the company's first design. (Alamy)

Austin Greyhound

In 1918, the RAF began the search for a replacement of the Bristol Fighter and issued a specification. A key requirement was that the replacement should be powered by a new radial engine, the nine-cylinder ABC Dragonfly developing 320hp (239kW). The Austin Motor Company was well used to aircraft manufacture, having been a subcontractor to the Royal Aircraft Factory for the S.E.5 and other types. The design submitted by Austin was a two-seat biplane of conventional all-wooden construction, with a cone-shaped cowling over the engine through which the cylinder heads protruded.

Three prototypes were ordered in May 1918. The first of these was constructed and tested but there were problems with the Dragonfly engine, which was overweight and underpowered and there were reliability issues. The second prototype was inevitably delayed and did not appear until January 1919 when it was delivered to the A&AEE. The third prototype was even further delayed, not being delivered for testing until February 1920. Performance was by then considered to be good, but no orders were placed. A Greyhound was used as a flying test bed until June 1922.

Armament fitted to the Greyhound comprised two synchronised Vickers machine guns and a single Lewis machine gun on a Scarff ring in the rear cockpit. The Greyhound had demonstrated a top speed of 129mph (208km/h) and a service ceiling of 19,000ft (5,790m). The wingspan was 39ft (11.89m) and its length was 26ft 8½in (8.14m).

The ABC Dragonfly-engined Austin Greyhound. (Picryl)

BAT F.K.25 Basilisk

By 1918, the Dutch aircraft designer Frederick Koolhoven had moved from Armstrong Whitworth to the British Aerial Transport Company of London. In that year, the Air Ministry issued a specification for a single-seat fighter for the RAF. It was to replace the Sopwith Snipe and a specific requirement was for the new aircraft to be powered by the 320hp ABC Dragonfly air-cooled radial engine, which was, as yet untried. With the benefit of hindsight, such a commitment to the Dragonfly appears to have been deeply flawed.

Three prototype Basilisks were ordered and built. The fuselage was a wooden monocoque construction and there were two Vickers machine guns mounted in front of the pilot, enclosed in a fairing that continued to form the coaming of the pilot's cockpit. This was quite a streamlined approach to what could otherwise be a drag-producing assembly.

The first flight of the first prototype was in September 1918. This aircraft was destroyed in early May 1919 while an attempt was made on the world altitude record. The engine caught fire and Peter Legh, BAT's test pilot, was killed after he jumped clear of the machine. Minor modifications were made to the second and third prototypes, and the second aircraft was tested by the RAF in October 1919.

Although not perhaps up to expectations, the Basilisk performance was good but it had become clear that the Dragonfly was hopelessly unreliable and no further development was planned. Frederick Koolhoven left BAT at the end of 1919 and the Basilisk project was abandoned.

The BAT F.K.25 Basilisk. (Nico Braas, 1000aircraftphotos.com)

Sopwith Snail

The Sopwith Snail was designed as a response to Air Ministry Specification A.1A calling for a light fighter aircraft with superior performance to the Sopwith Camel. Sopwith's designer, Herbert Smith, designed a biplane to be powered by the ABC Wasp radial engine, which delivered 170hp (127kW). An order for six prototypes was placed at the end of October 1917. These were to be constructed with conventional wooden frameworks, and be fabric covered. However, in November this order was changed to two prototypes each to have a plywood monocoque fuselage.

The first prototype was, in fact, built with the conventional wood and fabric fuselage and had its first flight in April 1918. The wings had a slight back-stagger with the pilot's head protruding through a cut-out in the upper wing. It was well armed with two synchronised forward-firing Vickers machine guns mounted within the fuselage, and a single Lewis machine gun fitted above the upper wing.

The second prototype had the monocoque fuselage, but the wings had conventional stagger resulting in the pilot being positioned behind the trailing edge of the upper wing.

Both of the prototypes were evaluated by the RAF. They were slightly faster than the Sopwith Camel, but handling was inferior and particularly so at low speeds. The ABC Wasp engine was proving unreliable, not just with the Sopwith Snail, and the competition to replace the Camel was abandoned in October 1918. The two aircraft were used as firewood in November 1919.

The monocoque Snail had a top speed of 124.5mph (108km/h). The wingspan was 25ft 4in (7.72m) and the Snail's length was 19ft (5.79m).

The Sopwith Snail fighter. (Johan Visshedijk, 1000aircraftphotos.com)

Westland Wagtail

Like the BAT Bantam and the Sopwith Snail, the Westland Wagtail was a response to the 1917 Air Ministry Specification A.1a for a light single-seat fighter. Particular emphasis was placed on manoeuvrability, rate of climb and the ability to achieve 135mph (217km/h) at a height of 15,000ft (4,570m) while carrying oxygen equipment and three machine guns.

The Wagtail was designed by Westland Aircraft of Yeovil, Somerset, and it was designed to be powered by the 170hp (127kW) ABC Wasp radial engine, as were its competitors. It was a conventional wood and fabric construction, with a large cut-out in the upper wing to improve pilot visibility. Two Vickers machine guns were mounted over the aircraft's nose.

In February 1918, an order for six prototypes was placed, although only four were constructed. The first airframe was used for structural testing. The Wagtail's first flight was delayed until April 1918 waiting for availability of the Wasp engine.

During tests against the BAT Bantam and the Sopwith Snail, also both Wasp powered, the Wagtail proved to have the best handling. However, the ABC Wasp engine was unreliable and it was abandoned in October 1918. The engine is noteworthy in being the predecessor to the equally unsuccessful ABC Dragonfly engine.

The Armistice in November 1918 halted any further interest in the fighter, but two Wagtails were used in 1921–1922 as test beds for the 150hp (112kW) Armstrong Siddeley Lynx radial engine.

With the Wasp engine, the Wagtail had a top speed of 125mph (21km/h) and a service ceiling of 20,000ft (6,100m). The wingspan was 23ft 2in (7.06m) and its length was 18ft 11in (5.77m).

The Westland Wagtail fighter. (Ray Watkins, 1000aircraftphotos.com)

Sopwith Bulldog

Sopwith Aviation Company began work on the design of a two-seat reconnaissance and fighter aircraft as a potential successor to the Bristol F.2 Fighter. The company was granted permission to produce two prototypes, designated Sopwith FR.2 (i.e., Fighter-Reconnaissance). The plan was to use the 200hp (149kW) Hispano Suiza 8 water-cooled engine, but it was in short supply and a switch was made to a new Clerget 11. This was an 11-cylinder rotary engine expected to produce 260hp (194kW).

In appearance, the prototype, now called the Bulldog, had a close resemblance to the first prototype Sopwith Snipe, although that aircraft was a single-seat fighter. The pilot sat under the upper wing with his head and shoulders protruding through a large cut-out in the upper centre section. The observer was in a cockpit behind the trailing edge and was equipped with two Lewis machine guns, one of these mounted on a pillar to give rearward defence, and the other on a telescopic mounting in front of the observer's cockpit. The pilot had two synchronised Vickers machine guns mounted in a hump in front of his cockpit.

The first prototype flew in early 1918, but was disappointing in terms of performance and handling. It was rebuilt with larger wings, which improved handling but made no difference to the poor performance. This was, in part, due to the Clerget engine, which only managed 200hp (149kW), far less than envisaged. The second prototype was fitted with the 360hp (267kW) ABC Dragonfly radial engine. Despite the high hopes that this engine would deliver excellent performance, it was hopelessly unreliable although performance was good when it worked.

Work on a third prototype Bulldog was abandoned. The second prototype continued to be test flown until at least March 1919 in the hope of solving the Dragonfly engine problems, but this ultimately proved futile.

The Bulldog with the Clerget engine had a top speed of 109mph (175km/h) with a service ceiling of 15,000ft (4,600m) and an endurance of two hours. Its wingspan was 33ft 9in (10.29m) and its length was 23ft (7.01m).

The Sopwith Bulldog with the troublesome ABC Dragonfly engine. (via Key Archives)

Armstrong Whitworth Armadillo

In 1917, Armstrong Whitworth's new chief designer, Fred Murphy, designed a radical-looking single-seat fighter. It was designed as a private venture although it met the requirements of Air Ministry Specification A1(a) calling for a replacement for the Sopwith Camel.

Armstrong Whitworth seems to have been more interested in seeing how the new design team tackled its work rather than producing a serious contender for what was clearly a key requirement. Either way, in January 1918, the company was granted a licence to build two prototypes.

The Armstrong Whitworth Armadillo had a square section fuselage with the engine enclosed by a circular cowl. There was a significant hump above the cowling that enclosed two synchronised Vickers machine guns. The aircraft was powered by a 230hp (170kW) Bentley BR 2 rotary engine.

The first prototype had its maiden flight in April 1918. The poor visibility from the cockpit was criticised and no formal evaluation of the Armadillo took place. By this time, the Sopwith Snipe had been ordered into production; it, had the same engine and was faster. The Armadillo project was abandoned and the second prototype was never completed.

The Armstrong Whitworth Armadillo had a top speed of 125mph (201km/h), a service ceiling of 24,000ft (7,300m) and an endurance of two hours 45 minutes. The wingspan was 27ft 9in (8.46m) and its length was 18ft 10in (5.74m).

Armstrong Whitworth's radical Armadillo. (Johan Visschedijk, 1000aircraftphotos.com)

Avro 533 Manchester

The Avro 533 Manchester was a development of the Avro Pike and 529A bombers. It was designed around Air Ministry requirements for a twin-engine bomber or a possible photo reconnaissance aircraft, with the new 320hp (240kW) ABC Dragonfly engine being specified.

The first aircraft framework was completed in October 1918, but the Dragonfly engines were delayed due to teething problems, and the first Manchester had two 300hp (220kW) Siddeley Puma water-cooled engines installed. The first flight took place early in December 1918 and was sent to No.186 Development Squadron at Gosport in Hampshire before moving to the A&AEE in March 1919. Trials lasted until September, when it was returned to Avro.

Delivery of the Dragonfly engines eventually occurred in December 1919. Following manufacturer's trials, this second prototype was flown to the A&AEE. Apart from the engines there were only minor differences between the two aircraft, all concerned with improving control.

The performance of both aircraft was not what had been expected, and production of the third prototype was abandoned before the proposed 400hp (300kW) Liberty engines were fitted. The Great War had also ended and the immediate need for bomber aircraft of this scale had evaporated. The prototypes were scrapped.

The Manchester had a maximum speed of about 125mph (201km/h) and a service ceiling of 17,000ft (5,200m). Its crew of three comprised the pilot, a nose gunner and a midships gunner; both gunners were equipped with a Lewis machine gun. Bomb load was up to 880lb (400kg). The wingspan was 60ft (18m) and the length was 37ft (11m).

The Avro 533 Manchester bomber; the name would appear again in the 1940s. (Johan Visschedijk, 1000aircraftphotos.com)

Westland Weasel

The Westland Weasel was Westland Aircraft's response to a Royal Air Force Type IIIA Specification for a two-seat fighter/reconnaissance aircraft as a replacement for the Bristol F2B Fighter. Westland received an order for three prototypes in April 1918. Other companies and aircraft being considered were the Bristol Badger and Austin Greyhound. All manufacturers were encouraged to offer the 320hp (240kW) ABC Dragonfly engine.

The Weasel was a conventional wood and fabric aircraft with the pilot and the observer/gunner in separate open cockpits, but seated close together. The upper wing above the pilot had a cut-out to improve upward visibility. The pilot was equipped with two synchronised Vickers machine guns and the observer with a Lewis machine gun.

By June 1918, Westland had largely completed the prototype, but was awaiting delivery of the engine. As a result, it did not fly until late November, by which time the Armistice had brought the Great War to an end.

The Dragonfly engine was no less a disaster for Westland than it was for so many other manufacturers. It was overweight, underpowered, unreliable, prone to serious vibrations and over-heating. These problems were never solved.

In tests, the Weasel displayed slightly better performance than the Bristol and Austin aircraft, but the failure of the Dragonfly engine and the lack of urgency to replace the Bristol Fighter meant that no production orders were to follow. However, a fourth prototype was ordered as an engine test bed. The first and third prototypes were fitted with the Armstrong Siddeley Jaguar engine and the second and fourth machine had the Bristol Jupiter engines installed. In this role, the last Weasel remained in service until May 1925.

With the Dragonfly engine, the Weasel had a top speed of 131mph (211km/h) with a service ceiling of 20,700ft (6,300m). Its wingspan was 35ft 6in (10.82m) and its length was 24ft 10in (7.57m).

The Westland Weasel. (Picryl)

BAT Bantam

British Aerial Transport Company employed Dutchman Frederick Koolhoven as a designer. His first design for the company was a single engine and single-seat fighter given the designation F.K.22. It was a conventional wooden aircraft. The expectation was that the F.K.22 would be powered by a 120hp (90kW) A.B.C. Mosquito radial engine, but this proved to be a failure. Instead, the first aircraft was fitted with a 170hp (127kW) A.B.C. Wasp engine, as was the third aircraft to be built.

The second F.K.22 had a 100hp (75kW) Gnome Monosoupape rotary engine. This was tested at the A&AEE in January 1918. The Air Ministry contract was for six aeroplane and Armament aircraft for development purposes. Three of these were slightly smaller aircraft, constructed as the F.K.23 Bantam.

Two more prototypes emerged of the larger aircraft and a further nine development machines followed. One was delivered to the Royal Aircraft Establishment in late July 1918, with the French Air Force and, eventually, the United States Army Air Corps received an aircraft for evaluation.

The small number of production Bantams required modification because of the unacceptable spin characteristics identified with the prototypes. Problems with the A.B.C. Wasp engine and the reduction in the size of the RAF following the Armistice, brought a halt to the life of the Bantam.

It had a top speed of 138mph (222km/h) and a service ceiling of 20,000ft (6,100m). Its wingspan was 25ft (7.6m) and its length was 18ft 5in (5.61m).

A BAT Bantam. (Alamy)

Short Shirl

In late 1917, the Admiralty issued a specification for a torpedo bomber capable of carrying and delivering the latest 1,422lb (645kg) Mark VIII torpedo. The Sopwith Cuckoo had been well received as a torpedo bomber but could not carry the new weapon.

Short Bros and Blackburn Aircraft Ltd submitted responses to the specification and both manufacturers were asked to build three prototypes using the 345hp (257kW) Rolls-Royce Eagle VIII, a water-cooled motor. Short Bros' offering was the Short Shirl, while Blackburn's was the Blackburd.

The Shirl had a plywood covered fuselage, more suitable than fabric for ditching in the sea should the need arise, and the undercarriage could be jettisoned for the same reason. Modifications were made to each of the first two prototypes, a slight sweepback of the wings on the first to counter a slight change in the centre of gravity following the fitting of flotation bags. The second prototype had larger ailerons and adverse changes to the tailplane, which were reversed in the third prototype.

Tests showed that the Shirl could indeed deliver the new torpedo, but after release of the weapon it lacked the agility of the Cuckoo. An order for 100 aircraft was placed, but in early 1919 it was cancelled. A single additional aircraft was eventually constructed for civilian use, bringing the total number of Shirls to four.

The Short Shirl delivering a torpedo. (Picryl)

Boulton Paul Bourges

In 1918, the Air Ministry issued a specification for a twin-engine bomber to replace the DH.10 Amiens. Interestingly, when the specification was issued the DH.10 had not yet entered service. In response, Boulton & Paul designed a twin-engined, long-range day bomber called the P.7 Bourges. Competitors were the Avro 533 Manchester and the Sopwith Cobham triplane.

In common with other manufacturers responding to the requirements of the Air Ministry's specification, Boulton & Paul selected the new ABC Dragonfly radial engine. The design impressed the Air Ministry and an order for three prototypes was placed 'off the drawing board'. The Bourges was a three-crew member aircraft armed with two Lewis machine guns, one in the nose on a Scarff mounting and the other in a dorsal position. A camera position was fitted just in front of the dorsal gunner's position, in recognition of a possible reconnaissance role. A bomb load of 900lb (408kg) of bombs could be carried in three cells with doors.

There were delays in the delivery of the Dragonfly engines and the first prototype was therefore fitted with Bentley BR-2 rotary engines, which were more reliable but less powerful. Thus equipped, it made its first flight in early 1919. At the end of May, the Bourges was demonstrated at Hendon showing excellent performance and manoeuvrability. It was fitted with the Dragonfly engines in July 1919 and again was capable of being looped, rolled and spun.

The second prototype had a 'gulled' upper wing to improve visibility and field of fire for the gunners in the nose and dorsal positions. It had the Dragonfly engines installed, but they were moved down onto the top of the lower wing, which required the undercarriage legs to be lengthened to provide clearance for the propellers. This aircraft was damaged in a crash later in 1919.

The third and last Bourges flew for the first time in December 1920. By now the reliability problems with the ABC Dragonfly engines had been fully realised, so this aircraft had the Bentley BR-2 fitted. Later, at the end of 1920 or beginning of 1921, it was again re-engined, this time with 450hp Napier Lion engines. It was flown with the original straight upper wing, and also with the gulled wing. This gave the Bourges the edge over its rivals, but by now the RAF had decided to cut costs and retain the DH.10. The third prototype was used for testing at the Royal Aircraft Establishment at Farnborough until 1924.

The Bourges had a top speed of 124mph (198km/h), a service ceiling of 20,000ft (6,095m) and an endurance of more than nine hours.

The Boulton Paul Bourges bomber. (Picryl)

Sopwith Snapper

The Snapper was developed in response to a 1918 Air Ministry specification for a single-seat fighter aircraft to replace the Sopwith Snipe. This was even before the Snipe entered service. There was almost certainly sense in this strategy of the Air Ministry to plan ahead. The German spring offensive, the Kaiserschlacht, began in March 1918, quickly pushing the Allies back to positions held in 1915. In addition, the Fokker D.VII started to appear on the Western Front in mid-1918. This was arguably the best fighter aircraft of the Great War. When the Air Ministry issued its specification of requirements, it had no reason to expect an end to the war during 1918.

As with some other Air Ministry specifications, a particular requirement was for the use of the ABC Dragonfly water-cooled radial engine. This engine had been ordered into mass production despite the fact that it had not been fully tested. The promises on which the judgement were made included excellent performance and ease of production. Sadly, the Dragonfly did not live up to its promises.

Sopwith proposed two designs. One of these was a triplane, the Sopwith Snark. The other was a biplane called the Sopwith Snapper. The Air Ministry ordered three prototypes of each aircraft.

The intention had been to construct the Snapper with a wooden monocoque fuselage, but for ease of construction a conventional wooden frame with fabric covering was substituted. Placing the cockpit behind the wings gave the pilot good visibility and two synchronised Vickers machine guns were positioned on the top decking of the fuselage.

The change of construction, coupled with development problems with the Dragonfly engine, delayed the build of the Snapper. It was not until May 1919 that the first prototype flew, followed by the remaining two aircraft. When the ABC Dragonfly engine worked correctly the performance was good. However, the engine problems were beyond solution and the engine contract was cancelled in September 1919.

This left Sopwith with three aircraft that could not be used for operational purposes, and following the end of hostilities, the demand for military hardware had entered a drought. The company tried to enter one of the Snappers in the 1919 Aerial Derby, a race sponsored by the *Daily Mail*. Although the aircraft was given a civil registration number and would be flown by Harry Hawker rather than a military pilot, the Air Ministry would not give permission because the Dragonfly was still classed as secret. The three Snappers were used for test flights at the Royal Aircraft Establishment until they were scrapped.

With the engine working correctly, the Snapper had a top speed of 140mph (230km/h) with a service ceiling of 23,000ft (7,000m). The wingspan was 28ft (8.53m) and the length was 20ft 7in (6.27m).

The Sopwith Snapper was a victim of the ABC Dragonfly engine. (via Key Archives)

Bristol Badger

The Bristol Type 23 Badger was designed as a two-seat fighter-reconnaissance aircraft towards the end of the Great War. Bristol had considered possible enhancement of the successful Bristol F2B Fighter by fitting a 200hp (150kW) Salmson radial engine, the 300hp (220kW) ABC Dragonfly radial or a 230hp (170kW) Bentley B.R.2 rotary engine.

In the event, Bristol chose to develop a new design using the Dragonfly engine. This design was drawn up in late 1917. Pilot and observer sat in tandem cockpits with the pilot under the trailing edge of the upper wing and the observer behind, equipped with a ring-mounted Lewis machine gun. The construction was the conventional wood with fabric covering. As initially envisaged, the Badger had virtually no fixed fin.

While detailed design work was taking place, it became apparent to Bristol that the ABC Dragonfly engine was proving to be unreliable and it would be prudent to seek an alternative powerplant. A local (to Bristol) company, Cosmos Engineering, was a manufacturer of aero engines and had produced a new 400hp (300kW) radial engine called the Cosmos Jupiter and this was considered as an alternative to the uncertainty of the Dragonfly.

Bristol was awarded a contract for the construction of three Badgers, two of these to be powered by the ABC Dragonfly, and one by the Cosmos Jupiter engine. In practice, it was the second Badger that flew with the Jupiter engine. The first Badger had its maiden flight on 4 February 1919. This flight ended in a crash due to fuel-supply problems. It was rebuilt, given a larger rudder, and delivered to the Air Board just 11 days later.

The Bristol Badger fighter. (Johan Visschedijk, 1000aircraftphotos.com)

The second Badger first flew on 24 May, but it was re-engined with the ABC Dragonfly and the Air Board acquired it in September 1919. This aircraft was fully armed with two fixed forward-firing Vickers machine guns and a single Scarff-mounted Lewis machine gun in the rear cockpit. It also had a larger fin to cope with the Jupiter engine's greater weight. The Badger suffered from aerodynamic problems caused by aileron drag. Because of this, the Air Board would not accept the third machine.

However, the Air Board was sufficiently impressed with the Jupiter engine that a fourth fully-armed Badger with this engine was ordered. Changes to the rudder and ailerons were made. This aircraft was loaned back to Bristol by the Air Board for development of the Jupiter engine during 1920–21. This aircraft was designated the Badger II.

With the 400hp (300kW) Cosmos (later Bristol) Jupiter engine, the Badger had a top speed of 142mph (228km/h) and a service ceiling of 20,600ft (6,280m). The wingspan was 36ft 9in (11.2m) and its length was 23ft 8in (7.21m).

The Bristol Badger displays its ABC Dragonfly engine. (Pictryl, public domain)

Airco DH.11 Oxford

The DH.11 Oxford was an Aircraft Manufacturing Company (Airco) twin-engined day bomber designed by Geoffrey de Havilland. It was intended as a replacement for the successful DH.10 Amiens, which was being manufactured in large numbers.

As required by the Air Ministry specification, it was designed to be powered by the as-yet-untried 320hp (240kW) ABC Dragonfly radial engine. This engine had been ordered in large numbers on the promise of excellent performance and was being specified for most of the new generation of aircraft on order for the RAF. It proved to be the death knell for many otherwise good designs.

The DH11 was a conventionally constructed wood and fabric aircraft with a deep fuselage, which filled the gap between lower and upper wings. It was an aerodynamically clean design, which was replicated with later de Havilland designs of the 1930s. The nose gunner and midships gunner had good fields of visibility. The gunners, equipped with Lewis machine guns, and the pilot all sat in open cockpits.

The first prototype had its maiden flight in January 1919 with the Dragonfly engines. The engines were far heavier than expected making the Oxford nose-heavy. They were also prone to over-heating, caused vibration and were very unreliable. They did not deliver the power that had been promised.

Two further prototypes had been planned, but these were cancelled in 1919 and no aircraft was selected to replace the DH.10 Amiens.

In addition to the Lewis guns, the Oxford could carry four 230lb (100kg) bombs internally. Its maximum speed was 123mph (198km/h) and it had a service ceiling of 14,500ft (4,400m). Its wingspan was 60ft 2in (18.34m) and its length was 45ft 2¾in (13.79m).

The Airco DH11 Oxford bomber. (Johan Visschedijk, 1000aircraftphotos.com)

Alphabetic Index of Aircraft

Manufacturer	Model	Page Number
Airco	DH1A	37
	DH2	38
	DH4	79
	DH3	129
	DH5	81
	DH6	66
	DH9	85
	DH9A	104
	DH10 Amiens	109
	DH11 Oxford	157
Armstrong Whitworth	Armadillo	148
	F.K.3	25
	F.K.8	76
Austin	Greyhound	143
Avro	501 and 503	123
	504	11
	529	138
	533 Manchester	149
BAT	Bantam	151
	F.K.25 Basilisk	144
Beardmore	WBIII	94
Blackburn	Kangaroo	103
	T.B.15	69
Boulton Paul	Bourges	153
Bristol	13 M.R.I	137
	Badger	155
	Boxkite	7
	Fighter F2B	67
	Scout	30
	Scout F	131
	T.B.8	14
Eastchurch	Kitten	141
Fairey	III	115

Alphabetic Index of Aircraft

Manufacturer	Model	Page Number
	Campania	75
	F.2	133
	N.9	140
Felixstowe	2A Flying Boat	83
	F.3	118
	F.5	98
	Porte Baby	70
Grahame-White	Type XV	10
Handley Page	O/100	53
	O/400	73
	V/1500	107
Kennedy	Giant	134
Martinsyde	S.1	23
	Elephant	60
	F.4 Buzzard	106
Nieuport	Nighthawk	120
Norman Thompson	NT.2B	95
	NT.4	96
Parnall	Panther	119
Pemberton-Billing	AD Flying Boat	97
	PB.25	46
Royal Aircraft Factory	B.E.2	9
	B.E.2c	26
	B.E.2d	27
	B.E.2e	44
	B.E.4	122
	B.E.8	17
	B.E.9	127
	B.E.12	64
	F.E.2b	47
	F.E.2d	48
	F.E.3	124
	F.E.8	52
	F.E.9	132
	H.R.E.2	126
	N.E.1	135
	R.E.5	40
	R.E.7	51
	R.E.8	62
	S.E.2	125

Manufacturer	Model	Page Number
	S.E.5a	87
Short	Bomber	55
	N.2B	139
	225 Seaplane	35
	S.38	16
	Shirl	152
	Type 320	92
	Type 827	41
Sopwith	807	43
	860	42
	Baby	33
	Bee	128
	Bulldog	147
	F.1 Camel	89
	2F.1 Camel	91
	Cuckoo	101
	Dolphin	99
	Dragon	121
	Hippo	136
	Pup	58
	Salamander	113
	Schneider	24
	Snail	145
	Snipe	111
	Snapper	154
	1½ Strutter	56
	Tabloid	18
	Three-seater	15
Vickers	Bullet	72
	F.B.5 Gunbus	20
	F.B.9 Gunbus	45
	F.B.12	130
	F.B.14	71
	Vimy	116
Westland	N.1B	142
	Wagtail	146
	Weasel	150
White & Thompson	No.3	22
	N.T. 3 Bognor Bloater	29
Wight	840	32
	Converted Seaplane	78
	Pusher Seaplane	28